The Daily Traditions and Supplications of The Prophet
(Peace Be Upon Him)

Authored by:
Dr. Abdullah Ibn Humoud Al-Furaih

Introduced by:
Prof. Dr. Khalid Ibn Ali Al-Misheigeh

 Contents

Table of Contents

Introductions

Topic	page
Foreword	19
Introduction	21
Preface	24
The meaning of Sunnah.	24
Some of the fruits of following the Sunnah.	26

Timed Sunan

Topic	Page
First Section of Timed Sunan: Before Dawn	30
First Section of Sunan Before Dawn: Upon waking up	30
The Prophet ﷺ would brush his teeth with a tooth-stick/brush.	30
The Prophet ﷺ would recite certain Adthkār upon waking up.	31

Topic	Page
③ The Prophet ﷺ would wipe his face after waking up.	31
④ The Prophet ﷺ would look at the sky.	31
⑤ The Prophet ﷺ would recite the last ten verses of Soorat of *Āl-'Imrān*.	31
⑥ The Prophet ﷺ would wash his hands three times.	32
⑦ The Prophet ﷺ ordered that one who wakes up should sniff water up the nostrils and blow it out three times.	32
⑧ The Prophet ﷺ would make *Wudū'* (Ablution).	32
▶ Some of the Sunan of *Wudū'* (Ablution):	33
① Using the Siwāk (Tooth-stick).	33
② Saying "Bismillāh" (In the name of Allāh).	34
③ Washing the hands three times.	34
④ Starting with the right hand side when washing the hands and feet.	34
⑤ Beginning by rinsing the mouth and sniffing water into the nostrils, before washing the face.	34
⑥ Exaggeration in sniffing water into the nose, unless one is fasting.	35
⑦ Using a single handful of water to rinse the mouth and sniff water into the nostrils, performing this three times.	35
⑧ Wiping the head in accordance with the Sunnah.	35

Contents

Topic	Page
⑨ Washing every organ of *Wudū'* three times.	35
⑩ Uttering the narrated supplication of Sunnah after *Wudū'*.	36
◆ Second Section of Sunan Before Dawn: Sunan of Qiyām Il-Layl (Voluntary night prayer) and Witr	37
① Performing Qiyām Il-Layl in its most recommended time.	37
② Praying eleven *Rak'ahs* of Qiyām Il-Layl.	39
③ Starting Qiyām Il-Layl with two short *Rak'ahs*.	39
④ Starting Qiyām Il-Layl with its specific introductory supplications.	40
⑤ Prolonging standing, bowing, and prostration, so that all of the pillars of prayer are approximately equal in duration.	41
⑥ Following the Sunan of recitation.	41
⑦ Making Tasleem (Salutation) every two *Rak'ahs*.	42
⑧ Reciting the Soorahs of Sunnah in the last three *Rak'ahs*.	42
⑨ Performing Qunoot in Witr prayer occasionally.	42
⑩ Making *Du'ā'* in the last third of the night.	44
⑪ Saying {سبحان الملك القدُّوس} "Glory be to the King and the Holy," three times, raising the voice in the third time.	45
⑫ Waking up the family members for Qiyām Il-Layl.	45

Contents

Topic	Page
◈ Avoiding overburdening one's self in Qiyām Il-Layl.	45
◈ Compensating for what was missed of the night prayer, next day during day time, but in an even number of Rak'ahs.	46
◆ Second Section of Timed Sunan: Fajr Time	48
▶ Section A of Sunan of Fajr Time: Sunan of Adthān	48
◈ Repeating after the *Mu'adthin*.	48
◈ Saying the narrated Dthikr after hearing the two testimonies performed by the *Mu'adthin*.	49
◈ Sending peace and blessings upon Prophet Muhammad ﷺ after the Adthān.	49
◈ Saying the specific Dthikr of Sunnah After the Adthān.	50
◈ Making *Du'ā'* (Supplication) after the Adthān.	50
▶ Section B of Sunan of Fajr Time: The Sunnah of Fajr	50
◈ The most assured of the daily Sunan is the Sunnah of Fajr.	51
◈ Characteristics of the Sunnah of Fajr.	51
▶ Section C of Sunan of Fajr Time: Sunan of Going to the Mosque	53
◈ Going to the mosque early.	53
◈ Going to the mosque in a state of purity, in order to have his steps record reward in his record and erase sins from his record.	53

Topic	Page
③ Going to prayer in a state of serenity and poise (dignity).	53
④ Entering the mosque with the right foot and exiting with the left foot.	54
⑤ Uttering the specific supplications of Sunnah upon entering/exiting the mosque.	54
⑥ Offering two *Rak'ahs* for greeting the mosque.	54
⑦ It is Sunnah for men to seek praying in the first row as it is the best row for men, while for women the best row is the last row.	55
⑧ Being close to the Imām.	55
▶ Section D of Sunan of Fajr Time: Sunan of Prayer	56
◆ Sunan of Sutrah (Screen in front of one who is praying)	56
① Taking Sutrah.	56
② Being close to the Sutrah.	57
③ Preventing anyone from passing in front of the worshiper.	57
④ Using the Siwāk (Tooth-stick) before every prayer.	57
◆ Sunan of the position of standing in prayer:	58
① Raising one's hands while making Takbeerat Al-Ihrām (i.e. saying Allāhu Akbar to begin prayer).	58
② While raising the hands to begin prayer, it is Sunnah to position the fingers extended straight and pointing upwards.	59

Topic	Page
③ Raising the hands to the position of Sunnah.	59
④ Placing the right hand over the left hand on the chest after making Takbeerat Il-Ihrām.	59
⑤ Holding the left hand with the right hand.	60
⑥ Starting prayer with the Introductory Supplication of Prayer after Takbeerat Il-Ihrām.	60
⑦ *Isti'ādthah* (seeking Allāh's refuge).	61
⑧ Basmalah (i.e. Saying {بِسْمِ اللَّهِ الرَّحْمَنِ الرَّحِيمِ} "In the Name of Allāh, the Most Beneficent, the Most Merciful.").	62
⑨ Saying "Āmeen" when the Imām completes reciting *Al-Fātihah*.	62
⑩ Reciting a Soorah after *Al-Fātihah*.	62
◆ Sunan of *Rukoo'* (The position of Bowing).	63
① Placing the palms of the hands on the knees and spreading the fingers out.	63
② Keeping the back straight while bowing.	63
③ Spreading the elbows away from the body while bowing.	64
④ Performing the specific supplications of Sunnah in *Rukoo'*.	64
◆ Sunan of the position of standing after raising up form *Rukoo'*.	65
① Prolonging this pillar.	65

Contents

Topic	Page
② To occasionally alternate between the various formulae of the specific supplication of Sunnah associated with the position of standing after raising up from *Rukoo'*.	65
③ Saying any of the additional supplications of Sunnah after the main supplication of raising from *Rukoo'*.	66
◆ Sunan of Sujood (The position of Prostration).	67
① Keeping a distance between the arms and the side, and between the thighs and the belly while prostrating.	67
② Ensuring the toes point towards the Qiblah while prostrating.	68
③ Saying the Adthkār of Sunnah in prostration.	68
④ Supplicating thoroughly in prostration.	69
◆ Sitting between the two prostrations.	70
① To place the left foot flat on the ground and sit on it, and place the right foot erect upright.	70
② Prolonging this pillar.	70
③ Briefly sitting for rest before rising up to the second and fourth *Rak'ahs*.	70
◆ Sunan of Tashahhud.	71
① Placing the left foot flat on the ground and sitting on it, and placing the right foot erect upright.	71
② Occasionally alternating between the forms of Sunnah regarding the position of the hands during Tashahhud.	72

Contents

Topic	Page
③ Occasionally alternating between the forms of Sunnah regarding the position of the fingers during Tashahhud.	72
④ Occasionally alternating between of the different Sunnah formulae of Tashahhud.	73
⑤ Sitting in the form of Tawarruk in the last Tashahhud of prayers comprising of three or four *Rak'ahs*.	74
⑥ Occasionally alternating between the different Sunnah formulae of the supplications of sending peace and blessings upon Prophet Muhammad ﷺ.	75
⑦ Seeking Allāh's refuge against four things before making Tasleem (Salutation, the last action in prayer).	75
◆ Supplications of Sunnah after obligatory prayers.	77
◆ Remaining seated after finishing Fajr prayer in one's place of prayer until the sun rises.	80
◆ Adthkār of the Morning (and the Evening).	81
◈ Dhuhā Time	86
◆ Ahādeeth that prove that Dhuhā prayer is Sunnah.	86
◆ The time for Dhuhā prayer.	87
◆ The number of *Rak'ahs* of Dhuhā prayer.	88
◈ Fourth: Dthuhr Time (Noon)	89
◆ The regular Sunnah before and after Dthuhr prayer.	89
◆ Prolonging the first *Rak'ah* of Dthuhr prayer.	89

Contents

Topic	Page
Delaying Dthuhr prayer when it is very hot, until it cools down.	90
Fifth: *Asr* Time	92
There is no regular Sunnah before *'Asr* prayer.	92
The time for Adthkār of the Evening (and the Morning).	93
Sixth: Maghrib Time (Sunset)	94
Preventing children from playing outside at this time.	94
Locking the doors at the beginning of Maghrib time and mentioning Allāh's name.	94
Praying two *Rak'ahs* before Maghrib prayer.	95
It is disliked to sleep before *'Ishā'* prayer.	96
Seventh: *'Ishā'* Time	97
Talking and gatherings are disliked after *'Ishā'* prayer.	97
It is better to delay *'Ishā'* prayer provided no harm is caused by this delay to the followers of the Imām.	97
It is Sunnah to recite *Soorat Al-Ikhlās* (Chapter 112) every night.	98
Sunan of Sleep:	99
① Locking the doors when going to sleep.	99
② Extinguishing the fire before going to sleep.	99
③ Making ablution before going to bed.	100

Topic	Page
④ Dusting the bed off before going to sleep.	100
⑤ Lying on the right side.	100
⑥ Placing one's hand under his cheek while lying down for sleep.	100
⑦ Saying the Adthkār of going to sleep.	101
▸ Adthkār of going to sleep, from the *Qur'ān*.	101
▸ Adthkār of going to sleep, from the Sunnah.	103
◆ Sunan of Dreams	106
▸ The Ahādeeth that illustrate the Sunan of dreams.	107
▸ Summary of the actions of Sunnah to be done on seeing good/bad dreams.	107
▸ The Dthikr of Sunnah that one should utter upon waking up during the night.	108

Contents

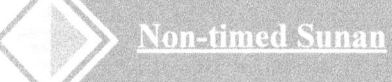 

Non-timed Sunan

Topic	page
First: Sunan of Eating	112
Saying "Bismillāh" (In the name of Allāh) before eating or drinking.	112
Eating from what is nearest to you of the dish.	113
Picking up a piece of food that has fallen, cleaning it, then eating it.	113
Licking the fingers after eating.	114
Cleaning the dish.	114
Eating with three fingers.	115
Taking three breaths outside the vessel during the course of drinking.	115
Thanking Allāh, the Almighty, after eating.	115
Gathering to have food.	116
Praising the food if you like it.	116
Making *Du'ā'* for the host.	117
Offering water to others, starting first with the one on the right hand side.	117
One who serves water to the people should be the last one to drink.	118

Contents

Topic	page
⑭ Covering containers and mentioning the name of Allāh when the night comes.	118
◈ Second: Sunan of Greeting, Meeting, and Gathering.	119
① Greeting others with Salām (The greeting of peace).	119
② Repeating Salām three times if needed.	120
③ Greeting those whom you know and those whom you do not know.	121
④ Initiating Salām according to the rules that the Sunnah illustrated.	121
⑤ Greeting children and shaking hands with them.	121
⑥ Greeting those at home upon entering home.	121
⑦ Lowering one's voice when greeting people if some of them are asleep.	123
⑧ Conveying greeting of Salām to others when asked by someone to do so.	123
⑨ Greeting people with Salām upon arriving at a meeting, and upon leaving.	123
⑩ Shaking hands and greeting others with Salām upon meeting each other.	124
⑪ Smiling.	124
⑫ Using polite and decent words.	124
⑬ Remembering Allāh in meetings and mentioning His name (i.e. praising Him).	125

Contents

Topic	page
Concluding meetings with Kaffārat Il-Majlis (i.e. Expiation of meetings).	125
Third: Sunan of Dress and Adornment	126
Starting with the right foot when putting shoes on.	126
Wearing white clothes.	127
Using perfume (for men).	127
It is disliked to refuse a gift of perfume.	128
Starting with the right side when combing the hair.	128
Fourth: Sunan of Sneezing and Yawning	129
Sunan of Sneezing:	129
Saying "Al-Hamdu Lillāh" (All praise is due to Allāh after sneezing, being replied "Yarhamuka Allāh", then replying "Yahdeekum Ullah wa Yuslihu Bālakum".	129
One who sneezes is not to be replied "Yarhamuka Allāh" except if he says "Al-Hamdu Lillāh".	130
Sunan of Yawning.	131
Resisting yawning as much as possible, or holding the hand over the mouth while yawning.	131
Fifth: Other Daily Sunan	132
Dthikr of entering and leaving the bathroom.	132
Preparing one's will.	133
Kindness and leniency in buying and selling.	133

Contents

Topic	page
◈ Praying two *Rak'ahs* after performing ablution.	134
◈ Waiting for prayer.	134
◈ Using Siwāk (Tooth-stick).	135
◈ Renewal of *Wudū'* for every prayer.	135
◈ *Du'ā'* (Supplication).	136
▸ Making *Du'ā'* while in a state of Tahārah (purity).	136
▸ Facing the Qiblah (Direction of the *Ka'bah*).	136
▸ Raising both hands.	136
▸ Starting *Du'ā'* by praising Allāh, the Almighty, then asking Allāh to send peace and blessings upon his Prophet ﷺ.	137
▸ Making *Du'ā'* with the ninety nine names of Allāh, the Almighty.	137
▸ Repetition and insistence in *Du'ā'*.	137
▸ Sunan of *Du'ā'* (Supplication).	138
◈ Remembrance of Allāh (Dthikr).	140
▸ Dthikr revives the heart.	140
▸ Allāh urges us in numerous verses to have the habit of remembrance of Allāh and mentioning His name (i.e. praising Him).	141
◈ Other Valuable Daily Adthkār of Sunnah	142

Foreword

Introduction of Prof. Dr. Khalid Ibn Ali Al-Misheigeh

In the Name of Allāh, the Most Beneficent, the Most Merciful.

All praise is due to Allāh alone, and may peace and blessings be upon the last Prophet ﷺ.

I had a look into this publication by Shaykh Abdullah Ibn Humoud Al-Furaih entitled المنح العلية في بيان السنن اليومية "*Al-Minaḥ Al-'Aliyyah fee Bayān As-Sunan Al-Yawmiyyah*" (i.e. The Supreme Blessings in Illustration of the Daily Sunan), and I have found it to be a very useful publication that gathered the verbal and physical Sunan of the day and night, whether independent or belongong to other acts of worship, that are proven by established evidence.

May Allāh reward him abundantly and cause benefit to prevail through this publication, Āmeen, and success is from Allāh.

Written by:

Prof. Dr. Khalid Ibn Ali Al-Misheigeh

7/11/1434 H.

Professor at Al-Qasseem University – College of Sharee'ah.

Teacher in the two Holy Mosques.

Introductions

Introduction of the Author

All praise is due to Allāh, Who says, "Indeed, in the Messenger of Allāh (i.e. Muhammad ﷺ [Peace and Blessings be Upon Him]) you have a good example to follow, for those who hope for the meeting with Allāh and the last day and remember Allāh abundantly." *(Soorat Ul-Ahzāb, Verse 21)*. Thus, Allāh has legislated following the Sunnah of the Prophet ﷺ. May peace and blessings of Allāh be upon the best of those who guided the Ummah to perfection of worship and compliance with the Sunnah.

Respected readers, I hereby place before you "The Daily Traditions of The Prophet PBUH", in which I gathered the daily traditions of the Prophet ﷺ (i.e. Sunan), since waking up from sleep in the early morning, until going to sleep at night, presented in sequence of time during the day. I then followed these by some other daily traditions of the Prophet ﷺ that are not related to a specific time of the day. By Sunnah I mean practices that are recommended but not obligatory; those which Allāh ordered us to perform to seek perfection and promote obedience.

This book is a summary of the original book entitled المنح العلية في بيان السنن اليومية "The Supreme Blessings in Illustration of the Daily Sunan". This summarized version simply presents each Sunnah along with its proof. As advised by some of our brothers, discussions of elaborated aspects of knowledge and detailed conclusions are omitted from this summarized version of the book. Thus, this book should help those who might not have the luxury of time or effort to read the original book, and should allow interested organizations of *Da'wah* to print and widely distribute the book.

Introductions

The purpose of illustrating the daily traditions of the Prophet ﷺ is to appropriately demonstrate his authentic traditions, which, unfortunately, have been misinterpreted by the West. In addition, we hope to remind those who abandon these traditions based on the argument that they are not obligatory, and help them avoid depriving themselves from the great rewards of performing these practices of Sunnah. I have done my best to illustrate these authentic daily traditions of the Prophet ﷺ along with their proofs and references, and I ask Allāh, the Almighty, to make us of the sincere followers of the guidance of the Prophet ﷺ, and of those who follow his trace and accompany him on the day of resurrection.

Written by the humble seeker of Allāh's Mercy,
Dr. Abdullah Ibn Humoud Al-Furaih
E-mail: A0504975170@hotmail.com

Introductions

Introductions

Preface

◆ The meaning of Sunnah:

Sunnah means what is liked and recommended in Islām.

Sunnah is that which is commanded in the *Sharee'ah* but is not obligatory. One who applies it will be rewarded and one who does not apply it will not be punished.

Examples of the eagerness of the Salaf (pious predecessors) to apply the Sunnah:

Introductions

 Imām Muslim reported through *An-Nu'mān Ibn Sālim* through *'Amr Ibn Awss* that he said, "*'Anbasah Ubn Abi Sufyān* told me in his illness in which he died about a Hadeeth so that he might be relieved by it. He said, 'I heard *Umm Habeebah* saying: I heard the Messenger of Allāh ﷺ saying,

"He who prays twelve *Rak'ahs* in a day and night, a house will be built for him in paradise because of them.".'." (Muslim no. 1727)

Umm Habeebah said, "I have never left them since I heard about them from the Messenger of Allāh, peace and blessings of Allāh be upon him."

'Anbasah said, "I have never left them since I heard about them from *Umm Habeebah*."

'Amr Ubn Awss said, "I have never left them since I heard about them from *'Anbasah*."

An-Nu'mān Ubn Sālim said, "I have never left them since I heard about them from *'Amr Ibn Awss*."

 'Aliy ؓ narrated that *Fātimah*, may Allāh be pleased with her, went to the Prophet ﷺ complaining about the effect of the stone hand-mill on her hands. She heard that the Prophet had received a few servants. When she came there she did not find him, so she mentioned her problem to *'Ā'ishah*. When the Prophet came, *'Ā'ishah* informed him about that. *'Aliy* added, "So the Prophet came to us when we had gone to bed. We wanted to get up on his arrival but he said, 'Stay where you are.' He then came and sat between me and her and I felt the coldness of his feet on my chest. He said, 'Shall I direct you to something better than what you have requested? When you go to bed say "Allāhu Akbar" thirty-four times, "Subhān Allāh" thirty-three times, and "Al-Hamdu Lillāh" thirty-three times, for that is far better for you than a servant.'."
(Al-Bukhāriy no. 3705, Muslim no. 2727)

In another narration, *'Aliy* ؓ said, "I have never left them since I heard about them from the Prophet ﷺ." He was asked, "Even on the night of the battle of Siffeen?" He said, "Even on the night of the battle of Siffeen."
(Al-Bukhāriy no. 5362, Muslim no. 2727)

It is known that *'Aliy* ؓ was one of the leaders in the battle of Siffeen, and despite being occupied with his role in it, he did not abandon this particular Sunnah.

Introductions

> *Ibn 'Umar* ﷺ used to lead the people in the funeral prayer and then he would get up and leave. He would not follow the funeral procession to the grave as he did not know about its virtue. When he was told about the Hadeeth of *Abi Hurayrah* ﷺ, he regretted it. So, imagine what he said?
>
> *Ibn 'Umar* threw the pebbles he had in his hand on the ground and said, "We missed so many Qeerāts." (Al-Bukhāriy no. 1324, Muslim no. 945)

An-Nawawiy said, "This Hadeeth reveals how eager the the companions were towards forms of obedience, and how regretful they were when they missed any act of Sunnah, even if they had not been aware of its virtues." (Refer to Al-Minhāj 7/15)

Some of the fruits of following the Sunnah:

> Respected reader, there are many fruits which result from following the Sunnah:

1. Reaching the stage of love, i.e. drawing closer to Allāh. By performing Nawāfil (Supererogatory Prayers), a believer attains Allāh's love.

   Ibn Ul-Qayyim, may Allāh have mercy upon him, said, "Allāh will not love you until you love His beloved Prophet, Muhammad ﷺ, both internally and externally, believe him, obey his commandments, reply positively to his call, resort to his judgment, prefer his love over the love of others, and prefer his obedience over the obedience of others. Otherwise, do not overburden yourself. Go back to your previous state, and try to find another light (pathway), because you are not on the straight path." (Madārij Us-Sālikeen, 3/37)

2. Gaining the company of Allāh, so that Allāh will guide one to the good. Accordingly, one's organs would only do what pleases Allāh Almighty, because if one gains Allāh's love, he will gain His company.

3. Having his supplications answered, which entails Allāh's love. One who draws closer to Allāh through voluntary prayers will attain Allāh's love, and he who attained Allāh's love will have his supplications answered.

Introductions

▶ The following Hadeeth indicates the above three fruits of following the Sunnah:

Abu Hurayrah reported that Allāh's Messenger said,

"Allāh, The Most High, says, 'He who is hostile to a Waliy (Companion) of Mine, I declare war against him. My slave approaches Me with nothing more beloved to Me than what I have made obligatory for him, and My slave keeps drawing closer to Me with voluntary acts until I love him, and when I love him, I become his hearing with which he hears, his sight with which he sees, his hand with which he seizes, and his foot with which he walks, if he asks Me I will surely give him, and if he seeks refuge in Me I will surely protect him.'." (Al-Bukhāriy no. 6502)

④ Compensating for any shortcomings incurred in the performance of the obligatory prayers.

This is indicated by the following Hadeeth:

Abu Hurayrah reported that Allāh's Messenger said,

"The first thing one will be called to account for on the day of judgment is his prayer. If it is found to be valid, he will be safe and successful, and if it is found to be invalid, he will be in misfortune and loss. If there were shortcomings in his obligatory prayers, Allāh will say to His angels (even though he already knows), 'See if my servant has voluntary prayers,' and the shortage of his obligatory prayers will be compensated with his voluntary prayers, then the rest of his deeds will be dealt with in the same manner." (Ahmad no. 9494, Abu Dawud no. 864, At-Tirmidthi no. 413)

Timed **Sunan**

Timed Sunan are the acts of Sunnah that are associated with specific times in the day and night. They are recommended to be performed in their specific times. They are divided into seven categories: Before dawn, dawn, forenoon, noon, afternoon, sunset, and night.

Timed Sunan

 First Section of Timed Sunan: **Before Dawn**

This is the time before Fajr when we wake up to perform Fajr prayer. The Sunan pertaining to this time are further divided into two sections:

 First Section of Sunan Before Dawn: Upon waking up

There are many traditions that the Prophet ﷺ used to do upon waking up from sleep, including the following:

 The Prophet ﷺ would brush his teeth with a tooth-stick/brush.

Hudthayfah reported, "When the Prophet got up at night, he used to clean his mouth with Siwāk." (Al-Bukhāriy no. 245, Muslim no. 255) In another narration reported by Imām Muslim, "When the Prophet woke up at night, he would brush his teeth with Siwāk." (Muslim no. 255)

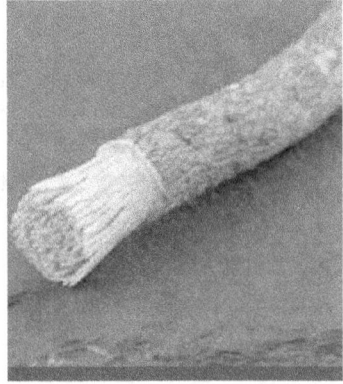

Timed Sunan

 The Prophet ﷺ would recite certain Adthkār upon waking up.

It is reported in Saheeh Al-Bukhāriy that *Hudthayfah* said, "When the Prophet ﷺ used to go to sleep at night he would say,

〈 بِاسْمِكَ اللَّهُمَّ أَمُوتُ وَ أَحْيَا 〉

'In the name of You, O Allāh, I die and I live,'

and when the Prophet used to wake up he would say,

〈 الْحَمْدُ لِلَّهِ الَّذِي أَحْيَانَا بَعْدَ مَا أَمَاتَنَا وَإِلَيْهِ النُّشُورُ 〉

'All praise is due to Allāh who has given us life after our death and to Him is the resurrection.'." (Al-Bukhāriy no. 6324)

It was also reported by Muslim in the Hadeeth of *Al-Barā'*. (Muslim no. 2711)

❸ The Prophet ﷺ would wipe his face after waking up.

❹ The Prophet ﷺ would look at the sky.

❺ The Prophet ﷺ would recite the last ten verses of The Chapter of *Āl-'Imrān* (Chapter no. 3).

The above three Sunan are mentioned in an agreed upon Hadeeth narrated by *Ibn 'Abbāss* who said, "I spent a night with my aunt *Maymoonah* the wife of the Prophet ﷺ, may Allāh be pleased with her. I lay down across the cushion and the Messenger of Allāh ﷺ and his wife were laying along it. The Prophet ﷺ slept until midnight, or a little before, or a little after, then woke up, and began to rub the sleep from his face with his hand. He then recited the last ten verses of *Soorat Āl-'Imrān*, then got up and went to a water skin that was hanging up and performed ablution from it, performing it well, and then he stood up and prayed ..." (Al-Bukhāriy no. 183, Muslim no. 763)

In another narration reported by Imām Muslim it said, "The Prophet ﷺ woke up near the end of the night, went out and looked at the sky, and then recited,

﴿إِنَّ فِي خَلْقِ السَّمَاوَاتِ وَالْأَرْضِ وَاخْتِلَافِ اللَّيْلِ وَالنَّهَارِ لَآيَاتٍ لِأُولِي الْأَلْبَابِ...﴾

'Verily, in the creation of the heavens and the earth, and in the alternation of night and day, there are indeed signs for men of intellect.' (*Soorat Āl-'Imrān*, Verse 190)" (Muslim no. 256)

 Timed Sunan

In Muslim's narration, it is illustrated that in order to practice this Sunnah one should recite the last ten verses of *Soorat Āl-'Imrān*, beginning at

﴿ إِنَّ فِي خَلْقِ السَّمَاوَاتِ وَالأَرْضِ وَاخْتِلافِ اللَّيْلِ وَالنَّهَارِ ﴾

until the end of the Soorah. (*Soorat Āl-'Imrān*, Verses 190-200)

6 **The Prophet ﷺ would wash his hands three times.**

Abu Hurayrah ؓ narrated that the Prophet ﷺ said,

"When any one of you wakes from sleep, he should wash his hands three times before placing them in a basin of water, because he does not know where his hands had spent the night." (Al-Bukhāriy no. 162, Muslim no. 278)

7 **The Prophet ﷺ ordered that one who wakes up should sniff water up the nostrils and blow it out three times.**

Abu Hurayrah ؓ narrated that Allāh's Messenger ﷺ said "When any one of you wakes up from sleep, he should sniff water into his nose and blow it out three times, for Satan spends the night in his nostrils." (Muslim no. 238)

In the narration of Al-Bukhāriy it reads, "When any one of you wakes up from sleep and performs ablution, he should sniff water into his nose and blow it out three times, for Satan spends the night in his nose." (Al-Bukhāriy no. 3295)

8 **The Prophet ﷺ would make *Wudū'* (Ablution).**

This is mentioned in the previous Hadeeth of *Ibn 'Abbāss*, may Allāh be pleased with them, which says that he ﷺ brought a water skin and made ablution out of it.

Timed Sunan

◈◈ Some of the Sunan of *Wudū'* (Ablution): ◈◈

We are briefly reminding of some of the Sunan of ablution, avoiding elaboration, as ablution is well known to all Muslims, just to make sure that the topic is covered within the topics of Sunan.

① Using the Siwāk (Tooth-stick).

It should be done before starting ablution or before rinsing the mouth. This is the second situation where Siwāk is recommended.

Abu Hurayrah narrated that Allāh's Messenger said, "If it was not for the fact that I may be overburdening my nation, I would have ordered them to use the Siwāk before every prayer." (Ahmad no. 9928, Ibn Khuzaymah no. 1/73/140, Al-Hākim no. 1/245, and it was also reported by Al-Bukhāriy)

In a narration of *'Ā'ishah*, she said, "We used to prepare his Siwāk and his purification water for him, and Allāh would cause him to wake whenever He, the Almighty, willed during the night, at which time he would use the Siwāk, perform *Wudū'*, and pray." (Muslim no. 746)

Timed Sunan

② **Saying "Bismillāh" (In the name of Allāh).**

Abu Hurayrah narrated that the Prophet said,

"There is no ablution for him who does not mention Allāh's name upon it." (Ahmad no. 11371, Abū Dāwood no. 101, Ibn Mājah no. 397)

③ **Washing the hands three times.**

'Uthmān described the Prophet's way of performing his ablution. He said, "The Prophet asked for water, then washed his hands three times ..."

'Uthmān said, "I saw the Prophet performing his ablution in the same manner as the ablution I am performing right now." (Al-Bukhāriy no. 164, Muslim no. 226)

④ **Starting with the right hand side when washing the hands and feet.**

'Ā'ishah, may Allāh be pleased with her, narrated, "The Prophet used to like starting with his right hand side first when putting on his shoes, combing his hair, purifying himself, and in all of his affairs." (Al-Bukhāriy no. 168, Muslim no. 268)

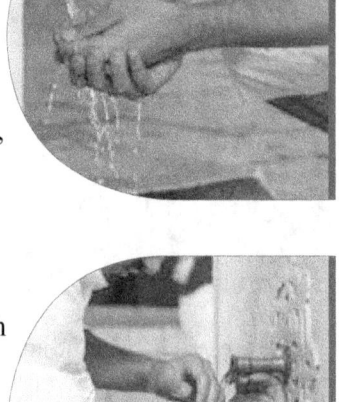

⑤ **Beginning by rinsing the mouth and sniffing water into the nostrils, before washing the face.**

'Uthmān said in his description of the *Wudū'* of the Prophet, "... and he rinsed his mouth and sniffed water into his nostrils and blew it out, then washed his face three times ..." (Al-Bukhāriy no. 199, Muslim no. 226)

If, however, one washed his face first and delayed rinsing his mouth and sniffing water into his nose until he completed washing his face, there would be no problem.

Timed Sunan

⟨6⟩ Exaggeration in sniffing water into the nose, unless one is fasting.

It was reported by *Luqayt Ibn Saburah* 🙏 that the Prophet ﷺ said, "Make *Wudū'* thoroughly, wash in between your fingers, and exaggerate in sniffing water into your nose, unless you are fasting." (Ahmad no. 17846, Abū Dāwood no. 142)

⟨7⟩ Using a single handful of water to rinse the mouth and sniff water into the nostrils, performing this three times.

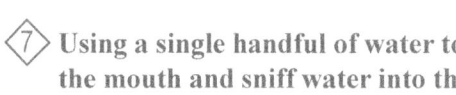

'Abdullāh Ibn Zayd 🙏 described the Prophet's ablution saying, "He put his hand into the vessel, rinsed his mouth, washed his nose with water and blew it out three times, with only one handful of water." (Al-Bukhāriy no. 192, Muslim no. 235)

⟨8⟩ Wiping the head in accordance with the Sunnah.

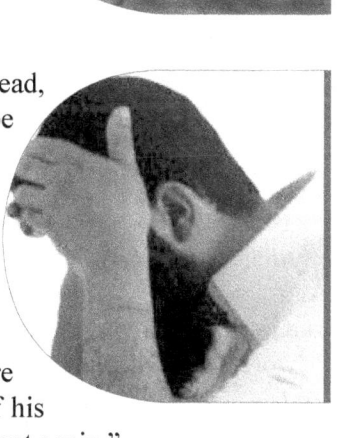

Using both hands, start at the front of the head, wipe all the way to the back of it, and then wipe back to the front of the head. A woman should do the same. However, she should not wipe her hair to the end of its full length.

This is proven by the following Hadeeth:

'Abdullāh Ibn Zayd 🙏 described the Prophet's ablution saying, "He wiped his entire head with his hands. He started at the front of his head, moved to the back, then returned to the front again." (Al-Bukhāriy no. 185, Muslim no. 235)

⟨9⟩ Washing every organ of *Wudū'* three times.

Washing once is obligatory, whereas washing three times is Sunnah, and one should not wash an organ of *Wudū'* more than three times.

Timed Sunan

This is proven by the following Ahādeeth:

Ibn 'Abbāss, may Allāh be pleased with them, narrated that the Prophet ﷺ washed every organ of *Wudū'* only once. (Al-Bukhāriy no. 157)

Moreover, Al-Bukhāriy reported through *'Abdillāh Ibn Zayd* that the Prophet ﷺ washed every organ of *Wudū'* twice. (Al-Bukhāriy no. 158)

It was also reported in the Saheehayn (The two authentic collections of the traditions of the Prophet ﷺ, Al-Bukhāriy and Muslim) through *'Uthmān* that the Prophet ﷺ washed every organ of *Wudū'* three times. (Al-Bukhāriy no. 159)

Accordingly, it is preferred to follow these different forms of *Wudū'* in different occasions. It is also allowed to wash the face three times, the hands two times, and the feet one time, as proven in the Hadeeth of *'Abdillāh Ibn Zayd* in another narration.

However, the practice of the Prophet ﷺ most of the time tended to perfection, washing every organ three times.

⑩ **Uttering the narrated supplication of Sunnah after *Wudū'*.**

'Umar narrated that the Prophet ﷺ said, "None of you makes ablution and completes it without uttering, 'I bear witness that none has the right to be worshiped except Allāh alone, and He has no partners, and I bear witness that Muhammad is His slave and Messenger,' except that all eight gates of Paradise will be opened for him, so he may enter from whichever gate he pleases." (Muslim no. 234)

Furthermore, it was mentioned in the Hadeeth narrated by *Abi Sa'eed* that the Prophet ﷺ said, "Whoever makes ablution and says, 'Glory be to You, O Allāh, and all praise is due to You. I bear witness that there is no God except You. I seek Your forgiveness and I repent unto you,' Allah will seal it with a stamp, then it will be raised under the Throne and it will not be broken until the day of resurrection. Allah will seal it with a stamp, then it will be raised under the Throne and it will not be broken until the day of resurrection." (*An-Nasā'iy*, Book of the Day and Night p. 173-174, *An-Nasā'iy* in As-Sunan Al-Kubra 6/25)

Ibn Hajar, may Allāh have mercy upon him, authenticated the Isnād (Chain of narration) of this Hadeeth and he said it is not classified as *Marfoo'*, but it is rather Mawqoof (Mawqoof refers to a narration attributed to a companion, whether a statement of that companion, an action, or otherwise). *Ibn Hajar* continues that, however, this does not harm the grade of the Hadeeth, which is considered to have an equivalent authenticity of a *Marfoo'* Hadeeth, because its content is not prone to accommodate the opinion of the narrator.

Timed Sunan

Second Section of Sunan Before Dawn: Sunan of Qiyām Il-Layl (Voluntary night prayer) and Witr

Qiyām Ul-Layl is voluntary night prayer.

Witr is voluntary prayer comprising of an odd number of *Rak'ahs* performed at night after *'Ishā'* prayer or before Fajr prayer.

1 Performing Qiyām Il-Layl in its most recommended time.

◆ Question:

What is the most recommended time to perform night prayer?

Answer:

The time for night prayer starts after finishing *'Ishā'* prayer, and lasts until dawn breaks. Thus, the time for Witr prayer is also between *'Ishā'* prayer and Fajr prayer.

 Timed Sunan

This is proven by the following Ahādeeth:

'Ā'ishah, may Allāh be pleased with her, narrated, "Allāh's Messenger ﷺ used to offer eleven *Rak'ahs* between *'Ishā'* and Fajr prayers. He used to make Tasleem (i.e. Salutation, the last action in any prayer, which involves saying "Peace and mercy of Allāh be upon you" and indicates the prayer is complete) and then would end with a single *Rak'ah*." (Al-Bukhāriy no. 2031, Muslim no. 736)

◆ **The best time of the night to offer night prayer is for a third of the night, starting at midnight.**

In other words, a Muslim should divide the night into two halves, and offer night prayer at the beginning of the second half for a duration equivalent to one third of the night, and then sleep in the remaining sixth of the night.

This is proven by the following Hadeeth:

'Abdullāh Ibn Amr, may Allāh be pleased him, narrated that Allāh's Messenger ﷺ said, "The most beloved fasting to Allāh was the fasting of the Prophet Dāwood, who used to fast every other day, and the most beloved prayer to Allāh was the prayer of Prophet Dāwood, who used to sleep the first half of the night, pray one third of it, and again sleep one sixth of it.'." (Al-Bukhāriy no. 3420, Muslim no. 1159)

◆ **Question:**

Hence, if someone wanted to apply this Sunnah, how would he calculate the night time?

Answer:

A person should calculate the night time from sunset until the time of appearance of dawn, and divide the night into six portions. The first three portions are the first half of the night. He should sleep in the first half of the night, then wake up to offer prayer for one third of the night starting at midnight, and then sleep in the remaining sixth of the night. Therefore, *'Ā'ishah*, may Allāh be pleased with her, said, "The Prophet ﷺ would always be asleep at the very end of the night (i.e. the last sixth of the night)." (Al-Bukhāriy no. 1133, Muslim no. 742)

Thus, it would be best to offer the night prayer as the Hadeeth of *'Abdillāh Ibn 'Amr* ﷺ stated.

Timed Sunan

▶ In conclusion, there are three grades of preference in regards to the time to offer voluntary night prayer:

Preference 1 (The highest in virtue): To sleep in the first half of the night, pray for one third of it, and then sleep in the remaining sixth of it, as has been illustrated in the Hadeeth of *'Abdillāh Ibn Amr* ﷺ.

Preference 2: To pray in the last third of the night.

This is indicated by the following Ahādeeth:

Abu Hurayrah ﷺ narrated that the Prophet ﷺ said, "Our Lord, Blessed and Exalted is He, descends every night to the lowest heaven in the last third of the night and says, 'Who is supplicating to Me so I may respond to him? Who is asking me so I may answer him. Who is asking my forgiveness so I may forgive him?'." (Al-Bukhāriy no. 1145, Muslim no. 758)

However, if someone fears that he might not be able to wake up later in the night, he can offer night prayer at the beginning of the night or at any time of the night that suits him, which is "Preference 3" that will be illustrated below.

Preference 3 (The lowest in virtue): To pray early in the night, or at any suitable time of the night.

This is proven by the following Hadeeth:

Jābir ﷺ narrated that the Prophet ﷺ said, "Whoever fears not to wake up at the last third of the night, let him pray at the beginning of the night, and whoever hopes to wake up in the last part of the night, let him pray at that time, as it is witnessed by Allāh and this is preferred." (Muslim no. 755)

What also supports this is the recommendation of the Prophet ﷺ to *Abi Dtharr, Abi d-Dardā'*, and *Abi Hurayrah*, may Allāh be pleased with all of them, as each one of them used to say, "My beloved one (i.e. the Prophet ﷺ) advised me to do three things, ..." one of which is, "... to offer Witr prayer before going to bed."

② Praying eleven *Rak'ahs* of Qiyām Il-Layl.

This is the complete form of voluntary night prayer.

'Ā'ishah, may Allāh be pleased with her, narrated, "Allāh's Messenger ﷺ would not pray more than eleven *Rak'ahs* in Ramadan or in any other month." (Al-Bukhāriy no. 1147, Muslim no. 738)

Timed Sunan

However, it was reported that the Prophet ﷺ offered thirteen *Rak'ahs*. This was reported by Muslim through *'Ā'ishah*.

These are various forms of offering Witr prayer. In general, the Prophet ﷺ would offer eleven *Rak'ahs* most of the time, and would rarely offer thirteen. In this way, the various Ahādeeth are reconciled together.

③ Starting Qiyām Il-Layl with two short *Rak'ahs*.

'Ā'ishah, may Allāh be pleased with her, narrated, "Allāh's Messenger ﷺ used to start his night prayer with two short *Rak'ahs*." (Muslim no. 767)

④ Starting Qiyām Il-Layl with its specific introductory supplications, among which are:

1> *'Ā'ishah*, may Allāh be pleased with her, narrated that whenever the Prophet ﷺ started his night prayer he would say, "O Allāh, Lord of Jibreel, *Meekā'eel*, and Isrāfeel, Creator of the heavens and the earth, Knower of the seen and unseen, You will judge between Your servants concerning wherein they differ. Guide me by Your grace to the disputed matters of truth. Indeed, You guide whomever You please to the straight path." (Muslim no. 770)

2> It was reported in the Saheehayn through *Ibn 'Abbāss* ﷺ that when the Prophet ﷺ used to pray Tahajjud he would say, "O Allāh, Our Lord, Yours is the praise. You are the light of the heavens and earth, and Yours is the praise. You sustain the heavens and earth and all that they contain. You are the King of the heavens and earth and all that they contain. You are the truth. Your promise is the truth. Your word is the truth. The meeting with You is the truth. Paradise is true. Hell is true. The Prophets are true. The Final Hour is true. O Allāh, to You I have submitted, in You I have believed, and upon You I rely. I repent to You. For your sake I dispute and by Your standards I judge, so forgive me for my earlier and later sins, for what I have committed secretly and what I have committed openly. You are my God. There is no God but You." (Al-Bukhāriy no. 7499, Muslim no. 768)

Timed Sunan

5 Prolonging standing, bowing, and prostration, so that all of the pillars of prayer are approximately equal in duration.

6 Following the Sunan of recitation, such as the following:

1. Reciting in a moderate pace, neither too fast, nor too slow.
2. Reciting verse by verse and avoiding joining two or three verses together without pausing at the end of each verse.
3. If one passes by a verse of praise he should praise, if he passes by a verse of supplication to Allāh, he should supplicate, and if he passes by a verse of seeking refuge in Allāh, he should do so.

The following Ahādeeth indicate this:

Hudthaifa said, "I prayed with the Messenger of Allāh one night and he started reciting Al-Baqarah. I thought that he would bow at the end of one hundred verses, but he proceeded. I then thought that he would perhaps recite the whole Soorah in a *Rak'ah*, but he proceeded, and I thought he would perhaps bow on completing this Soorah. He then started *An-Nisā'*, and completed it. He then started *Āl-'Imrān* and recited leisurely. When he recited the verses which referred to the Glory of Allāh, he glorified by saying 'Subhān Allāh' (Glory be to Allāh), when he recited the verses of requesting from Allāh he would request from him, and when he recited the verses of seeking refuge in Allāh he would do so. He then bowed and said: «سُبْحَانَ رَبِّيَ الْعَظِيمِ» 'Glory be to my Mighty Lord.' His bowing lasted about the same duration as that of his standing, and then on returning to the standing posture after bowing he would say: «سَمِعَ اللهُ لِمَنْ حَمِدَهُ» 'Allāh listens to him who praises Him,' and he stood about the same duration as that of his bowing. He then prostrated and said: «سُبْحَانَ رَبِّيَ الأَعْلَى» 'Glory be to my Lord, the most High,' and his prostration lasted nearly the same duration as that of his standing." (Muslim no. 772)

Moreover, Ahmad reported in his Musnad the Hadeeth of *Umm Salamah*, may Allāh be pleased with her, when she was asked about the Prophet's recitation and she said, "He used to break his recitation, verse by verse,

﴿بِسْمِ اللهِ الرَّحْمَنِ الرَّحِيمِ • الْحَمْدُ لِلَّهِ رَبِّ الْعَالَمِينَ • الرَّحْمَنِ الرَّحِيمِ • مَالِكِ يَوْمِ الدِّينِ﴾

'In the Name of Allāh, the Most Beneficent, the Most Merciful. All praises be to Allāh, the Lord of the *'Ālameen* (mankind, Jinn, and all that exists). The Most Beneficent, the Most Merciful. The Only Owner (and the Only Ruling Judge) of the day of recompense (i.e. the day of resurrection).' (*Soorat Ul-Fātihah, Verses 1-4*)." (Ahmad no. 26583, Ad-DāraQutniy 118)

Timed Sunan

7. Making Tasleem (Salutation) every two Rak'ahs.

Ibn 'Umar narrated that a man asked Allāh's Messenger ﷺ about night prayer. Allāh's Messenger ﷺ replied, "Night prayer consists of two Rak'ahs followed by two Rak'ahs, and so on, and if one fears that the dawn will approach (Fajr time), let him pray one Raka'ah and this will suffice as Witr for his prayer." (Al-Bukhāriy no. 990, Muslim no. 749)

This means that the Prophet ﷺ would not pray four consecutive Rak'ahs with one Tasleem, but he would pray two Rak'ahs and upon finishing them he would make Tasleem then pray another two Rak'ahs, and so forth.

8. Reciting the Soorahs of Sunnah in the last three Rak'ahs.

It is Sunnah for one to recite Soorat ﴿ سَبِّحِ اسْمَ رَبِّكَ الْأَعْلَى ﴾ in the first Rak'ah, ﴿ قُلْ يَا أَيُّهَا الْكَافِرُونَ ﴾ in the second, and ﴿ قُلْ هُوَ اللَّهُ أَحَدٌ ﴾ in the third.

This is proven by the following Hadeeth:

Ubayy Ibn Ka'b narrated, "The Prophet ﷺ would pray Witr and recite the Soorahs of ﴿ سَبِّحِ اسْمَ رَبِّكَ الْأَعْلَى ﴾ , ﴿ قُلْ يَا أَيُّهَا الْكَافِرُونَ ﴾ , and ﴿ قُلْ هُوَ اللَّهُ أَحَدٌ ﴾." (An-Nasā'iy no. 1733 and Ibn Mājah no. 1171)

9. Performing Qunoot in Witr prayer occasionally.

Qunoot is a loud supplication performed in the last Rak'ah of Witr. This is the Rak'ah in which one recites Soorat ﴿ قُلْ هُوَ اللَّهُ أَحَدٌ ﴾.

Occasionally performing Qunoot is Sunnah, and it is best to perform it sometomes ans leave it sometimes. This is the opinion of Ibn Taymiyyah, and some scholars prefer it to be left more often than performed.

Timed Sunan

◆ **Question:**

Should one raise his hands when making Qunoot?

Answer:

The correct answer is that one should raise his hands, and this is the opinion of the majority of the early scholars, may Allāh have mercy upon them.

This is proven by the Hadeeth of *'Umar Abn Il-Khattab* as stated and authenticated by *Al-Bayhaqiy*. *Al-Bayhaqiy*, may Allāh have mercy upon him, said, "A number of companions raised their hands while making Qunoot."

◆ **Question:**

With what should one start Qunoot?

Answer:

The preponderant opinion, and Allāh knows best, is that one starts by praising Allāh, glorifying Him, sending peace and blessings upon the Prophet Muhammad, then he makes the supplication.

This is proven by the following Hadeeth:

Fadhālah Ubn 'Ubayd said, "The Prophet heard a man making supplication without sending peace and blessings upon the Prophet. He said, 'This man was hasty,' and he called him. He said to him and to the others, 'When one of you makes supplication, let him start by praising Allāh, glorifying Him, sending peace and blessings upon the Prophet, then supplicate for whatever he wishes.'." (At-Tirmidthiy no. 3477 and he graded it as authentic)

Ibn Ul-Qayyim, may Allāh have mercy on him, said, "It is recommended for one making *Du'ā'* (supplication) to start by praising Allāh and glorifying Him, then to ask Allāh to fulfill his request, as the Hadeeth of *Fadhālah* stated. (Al-Wabil As-Sayyib, p. 110)

Timed Sunan

◆ **Question:** Should one wipe his face after finishing Qunoot?

Answer:

The correct opinion is that one should not wipe his face after Qunoot, as there is no authentic evidence that supports this action..

Imām Mālik, may Allāh have mercy on him, was told about a man who wiped his face after finishing *Du'ā'* and he disapproved it. He said, "I did not find anyone from the early generations doing that." (Rerfer to the book of Al-Witr by Al-Marwaziy, p. 236)

Shaykh Ul-Islam, may Allāh have mercy upon him, said, "As for wiping the face, there is only one or two Ahādeeth which cannot be used as decisive evidence." (Al-Fatāwā, 22/519)

10 Making *Du'ā'* in the last third of the night.

From among the assured Sunan is to make *Du'ā'* at the end of the night. If a person made *Du'ā'* in Qunoot at the end of the night, that would be enough for him. If, however, he did not, then he still has the opportunity to follow the Sunnah of making *Du'ā'* at the end of the night, as it is a time in which Allāh, the Almighty, descends in a manner befitting His Majesty to the lowest sky.

It has been reported in the Saheehayn through *Abi Hurayrah* ﷺ that the Prophet ﷺ said, "Allāh, Our Lord, Blessed and Exalted, descends every night in a manner befitting His Majesty, to the lowest sky during the last third of the night and says, 'Who supplicates to me so that I may answer him? Who asks me so that I may grant his request? Who asks my forgiveness so that I may forgive him?'." (Al-Bukhāriy no. 1145, Muslim no. 758)

Timed Sunan

 Saying {سبحان الملك القدّوس} "Glory be to the King and the Holy," three times, raising the voice in the third time.

This is proven by the following Hadeeth:

Ubayy Ubn Ka'b said, "The Messenger of Allāh used to recite {سَبِّحِ اسْمَ رَبِّكَ الْأَعْلَى} 'Glorify the Name of your Lord, the Most High,' {قُلْ يَا أَيُّهَا الْكَافِرُونَ} 'Say: O you disbelievers,' and {قُلْ هُوَ اللَّهُ أَحَدٌ} 'Say: He is Allāh, the One,' in the first, second, and third *Rak'ahs* of Witr consecutively. When he makes Tasleem from Witr he would say {سُبْحَانَ الْمَلِكِ الْقُدُّوسِ} 'Glory be to the King and the Holy,' three times." (Ahmad no. 15354 and *An-Nasā'iy* no. 1734, and authenticated by An-Nawawiy and Al-Albāniy)

In this Hadeeth, {سَبِّحِ اسْمَ رَبِّكَ الْأَعْلَى} refers to Chapter 87 of the Holy *Qur'ān*, {قُلْ يَا أَيُّهَا الْكَافِرُونَ} refers to Chapter 109 of the Holy *Qur'ān*, and {قُلْ هُوَ اللَّهُ أَحَدٌ} refers to Chapter 112 of the Holy *Qur'ān*.

Besides, in the narration of *Abd Ir-Rahmān Ibn Abzā*, the Prophet would raise his voice in his third time saying {سُبْحَانَ الْمَلِكِ الْقُدُّوسِ} 'Glory be to the King and the Holy.'.

 Waking up the family members for Qiyām Il-Layl.

It is recommended for both man and woman to wake their family members to offer night prayer, in cooperation to do good.

This is proven by the following Hadeeth:

'Ā'ishah, may Allāh be pleased with her, said, "The Prophet used to pray at night while I lay between him and the Qiblah. When he wanted to perform Witr prayer he would wake me up and I would perform Witr." (Al-Bukhāriy no. 512 and Muslim no. 512)

Besides, *Umm Salamah*, may Allāh be pleased with her, narrated that the Prophet once woke up and said, "Subhān Allāh! How many treasures and how many afflictions have been sent down tonight?! Who will wake up the sleeping lady occupants of these rooms (i.e. his wives)? A well-dressed soul in this world may be naked in the Hereafter." (Al-Bukhāriy no. 6218)

Timed Sunan

13 Avoiding overburdening one's self in Qiyām Il-Layl.

If one feels tired, he may sit down in his voluntary prayer.

Anass narrated, "The Prophet once entered the Mosque and found a rope hanging between two pillars. He said, 'What is this rope?' The people said, 'This rope is for *Zaynab*. She uses it while praying. When she feels tired she holds on to it to help her keep standing for prayer.' The Prophet said, 'Remove the rope. You should pray as long as you feel active, and when you get tired, sit down.'." (Al-Bukhāriy no. 1150, Muslim no. 784)

If one feels sleepy, he should take a nap, as this will help him regain his energy, and then he can continue praying.

'Ā'ishah, may Allāh be pleased with her, narrated that the Prophet said, "If one of you feels sleepy while he is praying, then he should rest until his sleepiness is gone. Verily, if one of you is praying while he is sleepy, he might not know if he is asking for forgiveness or cursing himself." (Al-Bukhāriy no. 212, Muslim no. 786)

The same also applies to someone who feels sleepy while reciting the *Qur'ān* at night. The Sunnah is to sleep so when he rises he will be more energetic.

Abu Hurayrah narrated that Allāh's Messenger said, "If one of you wakes up at night to recite the *Qur'ān*, and found it difficult to recite (due to sleepiness) and he cannot recognize his recitation, then he should sleep." (Muslim no. 787)

14 Compensating for what was missed of the night prayer, next day during day time, but in an even number of *Rak'ahs*.

If it was one's habit to pray Witr three *Rak'ahs* altogether and he was not able to offer them due to illness or sleep, it is Sunnah to offer them four *Rak'ahs* next day during daytime. If it was his habit to offer five *Rak'ahs* at night and he could not offer them due illness or sleep, it is Sunnah to offer six *Rak'ahs* next day during daytime, and so on.

'Ā'ishah, may Allāh be pleased with her, narrated, "If the Prophet felt sleepy or tired and could not offer the night prayer, he would offer twelve *Rak'ahs* next day during daytime." (Muslim no. 746)

Timed Sunan

Section of Timed Sunan: Before Dawn

 Timed Sunan

 Second Section of Timed Sunan: Fajr Time

There are numerous deeds that form part of the Sunnah of the Prophet ﷺ at Fajr Time.

 <u>Section A of Sunan of Fajr Time: Sunan of Adthān</u>

1 Repeating after the *Mu'adthin*.

It is Sunnah for one who hears the Adthān to repeat the same words of the Adthān except when the *Mu'adthin* says {حي على الصلاة} and {حي على الفلاح}, where one should say, "لا حول ولا قوة إلا بالله" 'There is neither power nor strength except with Allāh.'

'*Umar Ubn Ul-Khattab* ؓ narrated that Allāh's Messenger ﷺ said, "If the *Mu'adthin* says, 'Allāhu Akbar, Allāhu Akbar (Allāh is most Great, Allāh is most Great),' and one of you says, 'Allāhu Akbar, Allāhu Akbar,' then he says, 'Ash-hadu An Lā Ilāha Illa Allāh (I bear witness that there is no God worthy of worship except Allāh),' and one of you says, 'Ash-hadu An Lā Ilāha Illa Allāh,' then he says, 'Ashhadu Anna Muhammadan Rasoolullāh (I bear witness that Muhammad is the Messenger of Allāh),' and one of you says, 'Ashhadu Anna Muhammadan Rasoolullāh,' then he says, 'Hayya 'Ala As-Salāh (Come to prayer),' and one of says, 'Lā Hawla wa Lā Quwwata

Timed Sunan

Illā Billāh (There is no power nor strength except with Allāh),' then he says, 'Hayya 'Ala Al-Falāh (Come to success),' and one of says, 'Lā Hawla wa Lā Quwwata Illā Billāh,' then he says, 'Allāhu Akbar, Allāhu Akbar,' and one of you says, 'Allāhu Akbar, Allāhu Akbar,' then he says, 'Lā Ilāha Illa Allāh,' and one of you says, 'Lā Ilāha Illa Allāh,' from the heart, he will enter Paradise." (Muslim no. 385)

Note: When the *Mu'adthin* says, "As-Salātu Khayrun Min An-Nawm (Prayer is better than sleep)," one who is performing the Sunnah of repeating after the *Mu'adthin* should say "As-Salātu Khayrun Min An-Nawm," and this is called **At-Tathweeb**.

2 Saying the narrated Dthikr after hearing the two testimonies performed by the *Mu'adthin*.

It is Sunnah to say the following Dthikr after the *Mu'adthin* says, "I bear witness that Muhammad is the Messenger of Allāh," for the second time. *Sa'd Ubn Abi Waqqāss* narrated that the Prophet ﷺ said, "Whoever hears the *Mu'adthin* and says, 'Ash-hadu an Lā Ilāha Illa Allāhu Wahdahu Lā Shareeka Lah wa Anna Muhammadan 'Abduhoo wa Rasooluh. Radheetu Billāhi Rabban wa Bi Muhammadin Rasoolan wa Bil Islāmi Deenā (I bear witness that there is none worthy of worship except Allāh alone, with no partner or associate, and that Muhammad is the His slave and Messenger. I am content with Allāh as my Lord, Muhammad as my Messenger, and Islam as my religion),' whoever says this on hearing the Adthān, his sins will be forgiven." (Muslim no. 386)

3 Sending peace and blessings upon Prophet Muhammad ﷺ after the Adthān.

'Abdullāh Ibn 'Amr reported that Allāh's Messenger ﷺ said, "When you hear the *Mu'adthin*, repeat what he says, then send peace and blessings upon me, for whoever sends peace and blessings upon me once, Allāh will send peace and blessings upon him ten times. Then ask Allāh to grant me Al-Waseelah, for it is a rank in Jannah fitting for only one of Allāh's servants, and I hope that I may be that one, and whoever asks Allāh Al-Waseelah for me, my *Shafā'ah* (Intercession) becomes due to him." (Muslim no. 384)

The best formula of sending peace and blessings upon the Prophet Muhammad ﷺ is the Abrahamic supplication which is,

« اللهم صلِّ على محمد وعلى آل محمد ,كما صليت على إبراهيم وعلى آل إبراهيم ... »

Timed Sunan

"O Allāh, send prayers upon Muhammad and his family like You sent prayers upon Ibrāheem and his family ...", to the end of the Abrahamic supplication.

 Saying the specific Dthikr of Sunnah After the Adthān.

Jābir narrated that the Prophet said, "Whoever says the following after hearing the Adthān, deserves my *Shafā'ah* (Intercession) on the day of judgment:

« اللَّهُمَّ رَبَّ هَذِهِ الدَّعْوَةِ التَّامَّةِ، وَالصَّلَاةِ الْقَائِمَةِ، آتِ مُحَمَّدًا الْوَسِيلَةَ وَالْفَضِيلَةَ، وَابْعَثْهُ مَقَامًا مَحْمُودًا الَّذِي وَعَدْتَهُ »

'O Allāh, Lord of this perfect call and established prayer, grant Muhammad Al-Waseelah and Al-Fadheelah, and resurrect him in the praiseworthy position you have promised him.'." (Al-Bukhāriy no. 614)

Al-Waseelah is a rank in Jannah (Paradise) fitting for only one of Allāh's servants. Al-Fadheelah means virtue.

 Making *Du'ā'* (Supplication) after the Adthān.

'Abdullāh Ibn 'Amr narrated, "A man said to Allāh's Messenger , 'O Messenger of Allāh. The *Mu'adthins* are more privileged than us!' He replied, 'Say as they say and when you finish ask Allāh and He will respond to your request.'." (Abū Dāwood no. 524)

Moreover, it is narrated by *Anass* that the Prophet said, "*Du'ā'* made between the Adthān and Iqāmah is not rejected." (An-Nasā'iy no. 9895)

 Section B of Sunan of Fajr Time: The Sunnah of Fajr

It is one of the regular Sunan that a Muslim performs daily. It encompasses several other Sunan. Before presenting them, it is important to present the regular Sunan that are to be performed on a daily basis called "As-Sunan Ur-Rawātib", and they are twelve *Rak'ahs*.

Timed Sunan

Ummu Habeebah, may Allāh be pleased with her, said, "I heard the Messenger of Allāh ﷺ saying, 'Whoever prays twelve *Rak'ahs* in a day and night, a house will be built for him in Paradise.'." (Muslim no. 728)

In another narration by At-Tirmidthiy, he added, "Four *Rak'ahs* before Dthuhr, two *Rak'ahs* after Dthuhr, two *Rak'ahs* after Maghrib, two *Rak'ahs* after 'Isha, and two *Rak'ahs* before Fajr prayer." (At-Tirmidthiy no. 415)

It is preferred to offer the regular Sunan at home.

This is proven by the following Hadeeth:

Zayd Ibn Thābit ﷺ narrated that Allāh's Messenger ﷺ said, "O people, perform your voluntary prayers at your homes, because one's best prayer is the prayer he performs at home, except for the obligatory prayers." (Al-Bukhāriy no. 7290, Muslim no. 781)

① The most assured Sunnah of the daily Sunan is the Sunnah of Fajr.

This is indicated by the following Ahādeeth:

1> *'Ā'ishah*, may Allāh be pleased with her, said, "The Prophet ﷺ was not so much particular about observing any of the voluntary deeds as he was particular about observing the two voluntary *Rak'ahs* before Fajr prayer." (Al-Bukhāriy no. 1196, Muslim no. 724)

2> *'Ā'ishah*, may Allāh be pleased with her, said that the Prophet ﷺ said, "The two *Rak'ahs* of Fajr are better than the whole world and all that it contains." (Muslim no. 725)

② Characteristics of the Sunnah of Fajr:

Firstly, The Sunnah of Fajr is legal in both travel and residence. As for the rest of the Sunan, it is Sunnah to leave them out in travel, like the Sunan of Dthuhr, Maghrib, and *'Ishā'* prayers.

Secondly, Its reward is better than the whole world and all that it contains.

Thirdly, It is recommended to perform these two *Rak'ahs* short.

Timed Sunan

This is proven by the following Hadeeth:

'Ā'ishah, may Allāh be pleased with her, said, "The Prophet ﷺ used to perform the two *Rak'ahs* before Fajr prayer short that I would wonder whether he recited *Al-Fātihah* or not." (Al-Bukhāriy no. 1171, Muslim no. 724)

Yet, performing this Sunnah of making the Sunnah of Fajr short, should not lead one to hasten in his prayer to the extent that is prohibited.

Fourthly, It is Sunnah to recite the chapter of

﴿ قُلْ يَا أَيُّهَا الْكَافِرُونَ ﴾

in the first *Rak'ah* after *Al-Fātihah*, and to recite the chapter of

﴿ قُلْ هُوَ اللهُ أَحَدٌ ﴾

in the second *Rak'ah* after *Al-Fātihah*.

Alternatively, one can recite the following verse in the first *Rak'ah*,

﴿ قُولُوا آمَنَّا بِاللهِ وَمَا أُنْزِلَ إِلَيْنَا وَمَا أُنْزِلَ إِلَى إِبْرَاهِيمَ وَإِسْمَاعِيلَ وَإِسْحَاقَ وَيَعْقُوبَ وَالْأَسْبَاطِ وَمَا أُوتِيَ مُوسَى وَعِيسَى وَمَا أُوتِيَ النَّبِيُّونَ مِنْ رَبِّهِمْ لَا نُفَرِّقُ بَيْنَ أَحَدٍ مِنْهُمْ وَنَحْنُ لَهُ مُسْلِمُونَ ﴾

"Say O Muslims, 'We believe in Allāh and that which has been sent down to us and that which has been sent down to Ibrāheem (Abraham), *Isma'eel* (Ishmael), Ishāq (Isaac), *Ya'qoob* (Jacob), and to Al-Assbāt (the twelve sons of *Ya'qoob*), and that which has been given to Moosā (Moses) and *'Eissa* (Jesus), and that which has been given to the Prophets from their Lord. We make no distinction between any of them, and to Him we have submitted in Islam.'." (Al-Baqarah, Verse 136)

In the second *Rak'ah*, one can alternativelys recite the following verse:

﴿ قُلْ يَا أَهْلَ الْكِتَابِ تَعَالَوْا إِلَى كَلِمَةٍ سَوَاءٍ بَيْنَنَا وَبَيْنَكُمْ أَلَّا نَعْبُدَ إِلَّا اللهَ وَلَا نُشْرِكَ بِهِ شَيْئاً وَلَا يَتَّخِذَ بَعْضُنَا بَعْضاً أَرْبَاباً مِنْ دُونِ اللهِ فَإِنْ تَوَلَّوْا فَقُولُوا اشْهَدُوا بِأَنَّا مُسْلِمُونَ ﴾

"Say O Muhammad, 'O people of the Scripture (Jews and Christians), come to a just word between us and you, that we worship none but Allāh, and that we associate no partners with Him, and that none of us shall take others as lords besides Allāh. Then, if they turn away say, "Bear witness that we are Muslims."'." (*Soorat Āl-'Imrān*, Verse 64)

Fifthly, It is Sunnah to lie down on the right side after finishing the two voluntary *Rak'ahs* of Fajr.

'Ā'ishah, may Allāh be pleased with her, narrated that when the Prophet ﷺ completed the two *Rak'ahs* of Fajr, he would lie down on his right side." (Al-Bukhāriy no. 1160, Muslim no. 736)

Timed Sunan

Section C of Sunan of Fajr Time: Sunan of Going to the Mosque

This contains numerous Sunan:

Since Fajr prayer is the first prayer a man prays in the mosque during the day, the Sunan of going to the mosque will be presented here.

1 Going to the mosque early.

Abu Hurayrah narrated that the Prophet said, "If people were to know the virtues of At-Tahjeer, they would race one another for it." (Al-Bukhāriy no. 615, Muslim no. 437)

At-Tahjeer means going early to prayer.

2 Going to the mosque in a state of purity, in order to have his steps record reward in his record and erase sins from his record.

Abu Hurayrah reported that Allāh's Messenger said, "The prayer of a man in congregation is twenty-five times superior in reward to his prayer at home or in the market, and this is because he who performs ablution and perfects it, and goes to the mosque with the sole purpose of performing the prayer, he does not take a step without being raised a degree and having one of his sins erased. When he prays, as long as he is in the state  of purity, the angels keep on praying for him 'O Allāh, forgive him. O Allāh, accept his repentance,' and the angles continue this supplication for him as long as he does not do any harm and his ablution is not broken." (Muslim no. 649)

3 Going to prayer in a state of serenity and poise (dignity).

Abu Hurayrah narrated that the Prophet said, "When you hear the Iqāmah, walk to the mosque in calmness and poise, and do not rush to catch the prayer. If you catch it from the beginning that is fine. Otherwise, complete the *Rak'ahs* that you missed." (Al-Bukhāriy no. 636, Muslim no. 602)

Timed Sunan

Al-Imām Un-Nawawiy, may Allāh have mercy upon him, said, "The word Sakeenah (tranquility) mentioned in the above Hadeeth means to walk in calmness and avoid frivolity. Al-Waqār means behaving in dignity and poise, like lowering the gaze, speaking softly, and avoiding looking around with no reason." (Refer to the explanation of Muslim by An-Nawawiy, no. 602)

4 Entering the mosque with the right foot and exiting with the left foot.

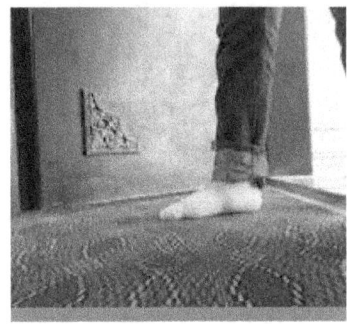

Anass said, "It is from the Sunnah to enter the mosque with your right foot and exit with your left foot." (Al-Hākim 1/338)

5 Uttering the specific supplications of Sunnah upon entering and upon exiting the mosque.

Abu Humayd or *Abu Usayd* narrated that the Messenger of Allāh said, "When one of you enters the mosque he should say:

« اللَّهُمَّ افْتَحْ لِي أَبْوَابَ رَحْمَتِكَ »

'O Allāh, open for me the gates of Your mercy,' and when he exits the mosque he should say:

« اللَّهُمَّ إِنِّي أَسْأَلُكَ مِنْ فَضْلِكَ »

'O Allāh, I ask You out of Your favors." (Muslim no. 713)

6 Offering two *Rak'ahs* for greeting the mosque.

If one comes early to the mosque, it is Sunnah for him not to sit down before offering two *Rak'ahs*. *Abu Qatādah* narrated that Allāh's Messenger said, "If one of you enters a mosque, he should not sit until he has offered two *Rak'ahs*." (Al-Bukhāriy no. 1163, Muslim no. 714)

Yet, offering any prayer on entering the mosque before sitting down would do for greeting the mosque. Thus, if one entered the mosque and prayed the two *Rak'ahs* before Fajr, Dthuhr, Dhuhā, or any other prayer, then whatever he prayed would count as greeting the mosque, because the purpose is to avoid sitting down before performing prayer, in order to have mosques maintained with prayer.

 It is Sunnah for men to seek praying in the first row as it is the best row for men, while for women the best row is the last row.

Abu Hurayrah reported that Allāh's Messenger said, "The best of the prayer rows for men are the first rows and the worst are the last rows, and the best of the prayer rows for women are the last rows and the worst are the first rows." (Muslim no. 440)

The best means having the greatest reward, and the worst means having the least reward.

This Hadeeth applies in the situation when men and women pray together with no separation. Thus, the last row would be the best for women, being furthest away from men's sight. However, if there was a barrier such as a curtain or a wall, or if there was a separate room for women, the best row for women in this case would be the first row, as they are already separate from men, according to the general reward of the first row as indicated by many Ahādeeth, one of which is:

Abu Hurayrah narrated that Allāh's Messenger said, "If the people knew the reward of answering the Adthān and praying in the first row in congregational prayer, and found no other way to obtain this reward except by drawing lots, they would do so, and if they knew the reward of offering Dthuhr prayer early in its specified time, they would compete for it, and if they knew the reward of *'Ishā'* and Fajr prayers in congregation, they would attend them even if they had to come to prayer crawling." (Al-Bukhāriy no. 615, Muslim no. 437)

 Being close to the Imām.

As we already mentioned, it is best to pray in the first row, and it would even be better to be closer to the Imām. Thus, the best position is the nearest to the Imām, whether from the right side or from the left side.

This is indicated by the following Hadeeth:

'Abudllāh Ibn Mas'ood reported that the Prophet said, "Let those of you who are mature and prudent be near me." (Abū Dāwood no. 674 and At-Tirmidthiy no. 228)

Timed Sunan

Section D of Sunan of Fajr Time: Sunan of Prayer:

◆ Your negligence of the congregational prayer deprives you of many virtues (rewards), even your steps towards the mosque elevate your status several levels in the sight of Allah and erase several of your sins.

◆ Prayer has many Sunan that a Muslim should eager to follow, presented as follows:

⟨1⟩ Sunan of Sutrah (Screen in front of one who is praying):

① Taking Sutrah.

It is Sunnah to take a Sutrah (screen) for the Imām (leader) in congregation, and also for one who is praying alone. However, those lead in prayer by the Imām do not need Sutrah, as the Sutrah of the Imām is sufficient for them.

Abu Sa'eed Il-Khudriy narrated that the Prophet said in a Hadeeth, "If one of you offers prayer behind something taken as a Sutrah ..." (Al-Bukhāriy no. 509, Muslim no. 505)

There are many Ahādeeth that talk about Sutrah being Sunnah. The Prophet used different forms of Sutrah such as a bed, wall, trunk of a tree, piece of wood, spear, goat, travel mount (camel), and so on.

Sutrah is permitted in both urban and rural/remote areas, in both travel and residence, and whether the person fears someone might pass in front of him

Timed Sunan

or not. The Ahādeeth did not differentiate between urban and rural areas, and the Prophet ﷺ used to take a Sutrah whether in travel or residence, as was reported in the Hadeeth of *Abi Juhayfa*. (Al-Bukhāriy no. 501, Muslim no. 503)

 Being close to the Sutrah.

The distance between one who is praying and the Sutrah is to be such that a goat could pass.

Sahl Ubn Sa'd Is-Sa'idiy narrated, "The distance between the place of prayer of the Prophet and the wall (i.e. Sutrah) was such that a goat could pass." (Al-Bukhāriy no. 496, Mulsim no. 508)

Imām Ahmad and *Abū Dāwood* stated that the distance between the Prophet ﷺ and the Sutrah would usually be about three cubits.

 Preventing anyone from passing in front of one who is praying.

Abu Sa'eed Il-Khudriy ﷺ reported that Allāh's Messenger ﷺ ordered that one who is praying should stop anyone from passing in front of him in order to preserve the sacredness of the place of prayer. (Muslim no. 505)

Moreover, a woman passing in front of a person who is praying should also be prevented as this would invalidate the prayer according to the Hadeeth of Muslim narrated by *Abi Dtharr*. The Hadeeth is reported by Imām Muslim in his Saheeh collection.

 Using the Siwāk (Tooth-stick) before every prayer.

This is the third situation where the use of Siwāk is recommended.

This is proven by the following Hadeeth:

Abu Hurayrah ﷺ narrated that the Prophet ﷺ said, "If it was not for the fact that I may be overburdening my nation, I would have ordered them to clean their teeth with the Siwāk before every prayer." (Al-Bukhāriy no. 887)

Timed Sunan

⟨2⟩ **Sunan of the position of Standing in Prayer:**

1 Raising one's hands while making Takbeerat Al-Ihrām (i.e. saying Allāhu Akbar to begin prayer).

Ibn 'Umar narrated the following Hadeeth, "When the Prophet stood to pray, he would start his prayer by raising his hands until they were the same height as his shoulders. When he wanted to bow, he would again raise his hands in a similar way. When he raised his head from bowing, he would do the same and say, 'Allāh listens to him who praises Him. O Allāh, praise be to You alone', and he would not do this in prostration" (Al-Bukhāriy no. 735, Muslim no. 390)

In his book entitled Al-Ifssāh, Ibn Hubairah, may Allāh have mercy on him, stated, "Scholars unanimously agreed that raising hands is Sunnah and not obligatory." (Al-Ifssāh, 1/123)

There are four positions in which the hands are to be raised, as mentioned in the authentic Ahādeeth.

> Upon making Takbeerat Al-Ihrām (saying {Allāhu Akbar} "Allāh is The Greatest" to begin prayer).

> Upon making *Rukoo'* (Bowing).

> Upon rising from bowing.

These three positions are proven by the Hadeeth narrated by *Ibn 'Umar*, may Allāh be pleased with them both, as mentioned previously.

The fourth position is:

> Upon standing up after finishing the first Tashahhud (Sitting).

This fourth position is proven by a Hadeeth narrated by *Ibn 'Umar*, may Allāh be pleased with them both, reported in Al-Bukhāriy's Saheeh collection.

Timed Sunan

 While raising the hands to begin prayer, it is Sunnah to position the fingers extended straight pointing upwards.

Abu Hurayrah narrated, "The Prophet ﷺ used to position his fingers extended straight pointing upwards when raising his hands to begin his prayer." (Ahmad no. 8875, Abu Dauwd no. 753 and At-Tirmidthiy no. 240, and authenticated by Al-Albāniy)

 Raising the hands to the position of Sunnah.

Narrations have proven that there are two ways of raising the hands according to the Sunnah.

In the Hadeeth of *Ibn 'Umar*, may Allāh be pleased with them, reported by Imām Muslim, it is stated that the Prophet ﷺ raised his hands up adjacent to his shoulders. (Al-Bukhāriy no. 735, Muslim no. 390)

In another narration reported by Muslim through *Mālik Ibn Il-Huwayrith*, the Prophet ﷺ is reported to have raised his hands up adjacent to his ears. (Muslim no. 391)

Thus, a person praying has the choice to raise his hands in any of the two forms, and it is best to alternate between both forms occasionally.

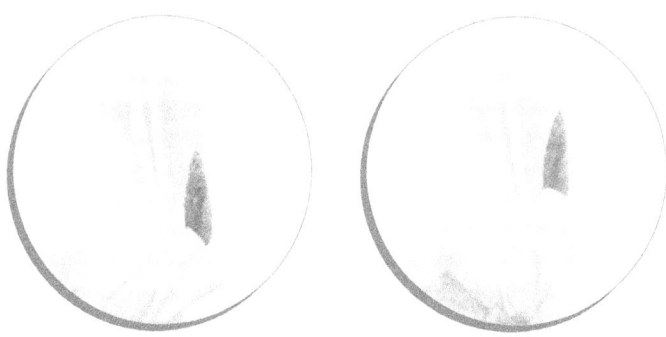

 Placing the right hand over the left hand on the chest after making Takbeerat Il-Ihrām.

Scholars unanimously agree on this, as reported by *Ibn Hubayrah*, may Allāh have mercy on them all. (Al-Ifssāh 1/124)

Timed Sunan

 Holding the left hand with the right hand.

There are two different forms for this, and it is recommended to alternate between both forms occasionally.

The first form is it to place the right hand over the left hand as proven by the Hadeeth reported by *Wā'il Ibn Hujr*  who said, "The Prophet ﷺ was seen placing his right hand over his left hand while standing for prayer." (Abū Dāwood no. 755 and *An-Nasā'iy* no. 888 and authenticated by Al-Albāniy)

The second form is to place the right hand over the left arm, based on the Hadeeth of *Sahl Ibn Sa'd* ﷺ who narrated, "People were ordered to place their right hands over their left arms while praying." (Al-Bukhāriy no. 740)

Thus, the worshiper could place his right hand on his left hand in one occasion and on his left arm in another occasion to diversify in applying the Sunnah.

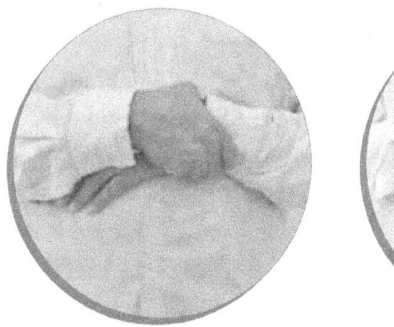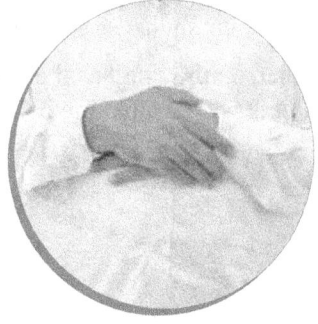

 Starting prayer with the Introductory Supplication of Prayer after Takbeerat Il-Ihrām.

This supplication has several formulae and it is recommended to diversify in using them. The worshiper could use a certain formula in one prayer, and another formula in a different prayer.

The following are some of the formulae of Sunnah for the Introsuctory Supplication:

» سُبْحَانَكَ اللَّهُمَّ وَبِحَمْدِكَ، تَبَارَكَ اسْمُكَ وَتَعَالَى جَدُّكَ، وَلاَ إِلَهَ غَيْرُكَ «

"Glory be to You, O Allāh, all praises are due to You, blessed is Your Name, high is Your Majesty, and none is worthy of worship but You." Narrated by *Abi Sa'eed* ﷺ. (Ahmad no. 11473, Abū Dāwood no. 776, At-Tirmidthiy no. 243, and *An-Nasā'iy* no. 900)

Timed Sunan

2⟩ « الْحَمْدُ للهِ حَمْداً كَثِيراً طَيِّباً مُبَارَكاً فِيهِ »

"Praise be to Allāh; abundant praise that is pleasant and blessed."

About the virtues of this supplication, Allāh's Messenger ﷺ said, "I saw twelve angels racing to write the reward of this phrase." (Muslim no. 600)

3⟩ اللَّهُمَّ بَاعِدْ بَيْنِي وَبَيْنَ خَطَايَايَ كَمَا بَاعَدْتَ بَيْنَ الْمَشْرِقِ وَالْمَغْرِبِ، اللَّهُمَّ نَقِّنِي مِنْ خَطَايَايَ كَمَا يُنَقَّى الثَّوْبُ الأَبْيَضُ مِنَ الدَّنَسِ، اللَّهُمَّ اغْسِلْنِي مِنْ خَطَايَايَ بِالثَّلْجِ وَالْمَاءِ وَالْبَرَدِ »

"O Allāh, distance me from my sins as You have distanced the East from the West. O Allāh, purify me from my sins as a white garment is purified from dirt. O Allāh, cleanse me of my sins with snow, water, and ice." (Al-Bukhāriy no. 744, Muslim no. 598)

4⟩ « اللهُ أَكْبَرُ كَبِيراً، وَالْحَمْدُ للهِ كَثِيراً، وَسُبْحَانَ اللهِ بُكْرَةً وَأَصِيلاً »

"Allāh is the most Great indeed. Praise be to Allāh in abundance. Glory be to Allāh, the Almighty, in the morning and in the evening."

Regarding the virtues of this phrase, Allāh's Messenger ﷺ said, "I was astonished by its effect! The gates of heavens were opened for it." (Muslim no. 601)

Moreover, there are some other formulae, some of which were mentioned earlier within the Sunan of Qiyām Il-Layl (night voluntary prayer).

7 *Isti'ādthah* (Seeking Allāh's refuge).

It is Sunnah and recommended to use different formulae of *Isti'ādthah* from time to time. Among the formulae of *Isti'ādthah* are the following:

1⟩ « أعوذ بالله من الشيطان الرجيم »

"I seek refuge in Allāh against the cursed devil."

This is the formula that most scholars, may Allāh have mercy on them, chose, and Allāh, the Almighty, said regarding this formula:

﴿ فَإِذَا قَرَأْتَ الْقُرْآنَ فَاسْتَعِذْ بِاللَّهِ مِنَ الشَّيْطَانِ الرَّجِيمِ ﴾ [النحل : 98]

"So when you want to recite the *Qur'ān*, seek refuge in Allāh from the cursed Satan." (*Soorat Un-Nahl*, Verse 98)

Timed Sunan

②

« أعوذ بالله السميع العليم من الشيطان الرجيم »

"I seek refuge in Allāh, the All-Hearer, the All-Knower, against the cursed devil."

Allāh, the Almighty, says regarding this formula:

﴿ وَإِمَّا يَنزَغَنَّكَ مِنَ ٱلشَّيْطَٰنِ نَزْغٌ فَٱسْتَعِذْ بِٱللَّهِ ۚ إِنَّهُۥ هُوَ ٱلسَّمِيعُ ٱلْعَلِيمُ ﴾

"And if an evil whisper from Satan tries to turn you away, O Muhammad, from doing good, etc., then seek refuge in Allāh. Verily, He is the All-Hearer, the All-Knower." (*Soorat Fussilat*, Verse 36)

8 Basmalah (i.e. Saying ﴿بِسْمِ ٱللَّهِ ٱلرَّحْمَٰنِ ٱلرَّحِيمِ﴾ "In the Name of Allāh, the Most Beneficent, the Most Merciful.").

It is Sunnah to say Basmalah after *Isti'ādthah*. Basmalah is to say, "In the Name of Allāh, the Most Beneficent, the Most Merciful."

Nu'aim Ul-Mujmir ❀ narrated, "I prayed behind *Abi Hurayrah* and he recited, 'In the Name of Allāh, the Most Gracious, the Most Merciful,' then he recited *Umm Al-Qur'ān* (*Al-Fātihah*) ... ," and at the end of the Hadeeth he said, "By the One in Whose Hand is my soul, my prayer most closely resembles the prayer of the Messenger of Allāh." (*An-Nasā'iy* no. 906)

What this shows is that it is not obligatory, which is also indicated by the Hadeeth narrated by *Abi Hurayrah* ❀ that narrates the situation when the Prophet ﷺ taught the man who was making some mistakes in his prayer. (Al-Bukhāriy no. 757, Muslim no. 397)

9 Saying "Āmeen" when the Imām completes reciting *Al-Fātihah*.

It is Sunnah to say "Āmeen" when the Imām completes *Al-Fātihah* in loud prayers. *Abu Hurayrah* ❀ narrated that the Prophet ﷺ said, "Say Āmeen when the Imām says it, and if one of you said it in harmony with that of the angels, then all his past sins will be forgiven." (Al-Bukhāriy no. 780, Muslim no. 410)

The meaning of "Āmeen" is, 'O Allāh, respond to our supplication.'

10 Reciting a Soorah after *Al-Fātihah*.

Reciting a Soorah after *Al-Fātihah* is Sunnah in the first two *Rak'ahs*, as agreed upon by the majority of scholars, may Allāh have mercy on them all. *Abu Qatādah* ❀ narrated, "The Messenger of Allāh ﷺ used to recite *Soorat Al-Fātihah* followed by another Soorah in the first two *Rak'ahs* of Dthuhr

Timed Sunan

prayer, and he would prolong the first *Rak'ah* more than the second." (Al-Bukhāriy no. 759, Muslim no. 451)

After reciting *Al-Fātihah* with the Imām, one should listen to the recitation of the Imām after *Al-Fātihah* in loud prayers.

Ibn Qudāmah said, "Scholars unanimously agreed on the fact that it is Sunnah to recite a Soorah after *Al-Fātihah* in the first two *Rak'ahs* of every prayer." (Al-Mughny 1/568)

⟨3⟩ Sunan of *Rukoo'* (Bowing):

1 Placing the palms of the hands on the knees and spreading the fingers out.

Abu Humayd Is-Sā'idiy ؓ narrated, "I am the most knowledgeable of you about the prayer of the Messenger of Allāh ﷺ. I saw him raise his hands adjacent to his shoulders while saying "Allāhu Akbar" to begin his prayer, and when he bowed, he firmly placed the palms of his hands on his knees … ," to the end of the Hadeeth. (Al-Bukhāriy no. 828)

Furthermore, *Abu Mas'ood* ؓ reported, "… and he spread his fingers out around his knees …" (Ahmad no. 17081, Abū Dāwood no. 863 and *An-Nasā'iy* no. 1038)

2 Keeping the back straight while bowing.

This is indicated by the Hadeeth of *Abi Humayd* ؓ in which he reported, "… and when he bowed down he would firmly place his palms on his knees and bend down keeping his back straight during bowing …" (Al-Bukhāriy no. 828)

Namely, he would bow down with his back straight and avoid his back taking the shape of an arch, and his head would be on the same level with his back, neither higher or lower, as *'Ā'ishah*, may Allāh be pleased with her, narrated in the following Hadeeth reported by Muslim:

Timed Sunan

"When the Prophet ﷺ made *Rukoo'*, he would neither raise his head nor lower it, but he would keep it in a position between both." (Muslim no. 498)

 Spreading the elbows away from the body while bowing.

What proves this is the Hadeeth of *Abi Mas'ood* ﷺ who narrated, "Then he bowed down, spread his elbows away from his body, placed his palms on his knees, spread his fingers out." He said, "I saw the Prophet praying like this.". (Ahmad no. 17081, Abū Dāwood no. 863 and *An-Nasā'iy* no. 1038)

However, this is on condition that the worshiper should not harm those who stand beside him/her.

An-Nawawiy, may Allāh have mercy on him, said, "The scholars agreed that spreading the elbows away from the body while bowing is recommended, and I did not see anyone who opposed this opinion. Al-Imām At-Tirmidthiy also reported that it is recommended in both bowing and prostration, and that this is the opinion of the scholars in general." (*Al-Majmoo'*, 3/410)

 Performing the specific supplications of Sunnah in *Rukoo'*.

After saying {سبحان ربي العظيم} "Glory be to my Lord the Almighty", some other supplications can be said, and these include:

1﹥
« سُبْحَانَكَ اللَّهُمَّ رَبَّنَا وَبِحَمْدِكَ، اللَّهُمَّ اغْفِرْ لِي »

"O Allāh, Glory and Praise be to you. O Allāh, forgive me." This supplication was narrated in the Hadeeth of *'Ā'ishah*, may Allāh be pleased with her. (Al-Bukhāriy no. 794, Muslim no.484)

2﹥
« سُبُّوحٌ قُدُّوسٌ رَبُّ الْمَلَائِكَةِ وَالرُّوحِ »

All-Glorious, All-Holy, Lord of the angels and spirit." This supplication was also narrated in the Hadeeth of *'Ā'ishah*, may Allāh be pleased with her. (Muslim no. 487)

3﹥
« اللَّهُمَّ لَكَ رَكَعْتُ، وَبِكَ آمَنْتُ، وَلَكَ أَسْلَمْتُ، خَشَعَ لَكَ سَمْعِي، وَبَصَرِي، وَمُخِّي، وَعَظْمِي، وَعَصَبِي »

Timed Sunan

"O Allāh, it is for You that I bowed. I affirm my faith in You and I submit to You. My hearing, my eyesight, my marrow, my bone, and my sinew are all humbled to you."

This supplication was narrated in the Hadeeth of *'Aliy* ﷺ. (Muslim no. 771)

4⟩

« سبحانَ ذِي الجَبَرُوتِ وَالمَلَكُوتِ وَالكِبْرِياءِ وَالعَظَمَة »

"Glory be to the One who has all Power, all of the Kingdom, all Pride, and all Greatness." (Ahmad no. 23411, Abū Dāwood no. 873 and An-Nasā'iy no. 1050)

⟨4⟩ **Sunan of the position of standing after raising up form *Rukoo'*:**

① **Prolonging this pillar.**

Thābit Ul-Banāni narrated through Anass ﷺ that he said, "I make sure to lead you in prayer in a way that resembles the way the Prophet led us in prayer." *Thābit Ul-Banāni* said, "*Anass* was doing something that you do not do. When he raised from *Rukoo'*, he would stay for a while to the extent that someone might say he forgot. When he raised his head after finishing prostration, he would also stay for a while to the extent that someone might say he forgot." (Al-Bukhāriy no. 821, Muslim no. 472)

② To occasionally alternate between the various formulae of the specific supplication of Sunnah associated with the position of standing after raising up from *Rukoo'*, which include:

1⟩

« اللَّهُمَّ رَبَّنَا وَلَكَ الْحَمْدُ »

"O Allāh our Lord, and Praise is due to you." Reported by Al-Bukhāriy through *Abi Hurayrah* ﷺ. (Al-Bukhāriy no. 795)

2⟩

« اللَّهُمَّ رَبَّنَا لَكَ الْحَمْدُ »

"O Allāh our Lord, Praise is due to You." Reported in an agreed upon Hadeeth narrated by *Abi Hurayrah* ﷺ. (Al-Bukhāriy no. 796, Muslim no. 404)

Timed Sunan

3 ⟩

« رَبَّنَا وَلَكَ الْحَمْدُ »

"O Our Lord, and Praise is due to You." Reported in an agreed upon Hadeeth narrated through *'Ā'ishah*, may Allāh be pleased with her. (Al-Bukhāriy no. 799, Muslim no. 411)

4 ⟩

« رَبَّنَا لَكَ الْحَمْدُ »

"O Our Lord, Praise is due to You." Narrated by Al-Bukhāriy through *Abi Hurayrah* ﷺ. (Al-Bukhāriy no. 722)

Thus, any of the above-mentioned formulae can be used, and it is best to occasionally alternate between these formulae to diversify one's Dthikr.

3 Saying any of the additional supplications of Sunnah after the main supplication of raising from *Rukoo'*:

1 ⟩

« رَبَّنَا لَكَ الْحَمْدُ، مِلْءُ السَّمَاوَاتِ وَالْأَرْضِ، وَمِلْءُ مَا شِئْتَ مِنْ شَيْءٍ بَعْدُ، أَهْلَ الثَّنَاءِ وَالْمَجْدِ، أَحَقُّ مَا قَالَ الْعَبْدُ، وَكُلُّنَا لَكَ عَبْدٌ، اللَّهُمَّ لَا مَانِعَ لِمَا أَعْطَيْتَ، وَلَا مُعْطِيَ لِمَا مَنَعْتَ، وَلَا يَنْفَعُ ذَا الْجَدِّ مِنْكَ الْجَدُّ »

"O Allāh our Lord, to You be the Praise that would fill all the heavens and the earth, and all that pleases You besides them. O Possessor of Praise and Majesty, the truest thing a servant has said, and we are all Your servants. O Allāh, none can prevent what You have willed to bestow, and none can give what You hold back, and hard efforts by anyone cannot benefit one against Your Will." The Hadeeth is reported by Muslim through *Abi Sa'eed Il-Khudriy* ﷺ. (Muslim no. 477)

2 ⟩

« الْحَمْدُ لِلَّهِ حَمْداً كَثِيراً طَيِّباً مُبَارَكاً فِيهِ »

"Praise be to Allāh; abundant praise that is pleasant and blessed." The Messenger of Allāh ﷺ said, "I saw twelve angels racing one another to take this supplication up (to Allāh)." (Al-Bukhāriy no. 799, Muslim no. 600)

3 ⟩

« اللَّهُمَّ طَهِّرْنِي بِالثَّلْجِ وَالْبَرَدِ وَالْمَاءِ الْبَارِدِ، اللَّهُمَّ طَهِّرْنِي مِنَ الذُّنُوبِ وَالْخَطَايَا كَمَا يُنَقَّى الثَّوْبُ الْأَبْيَضُ مِنَ الْوَسَخِ »

"O Allāh, wash my sins with snow, hail, and cold water. O Allāh, cleanse me from my sins like a white garment is purified from dirt." (Muslim no. 476)

Timed Sunan

If a Muslim says these supplications, he can prolong the time he spends performing this pillar of prayer (Standing up after raising from *Rukoo'*).

⟨5⟩ **Sunan of Sujood (The position of Prostration).**

1 Keeping a distance between the arms and the side, and between the thighs and the belly while prostrating.

'*Abdullāh Ibn Baheenah* narrated, "When the Prophet prostrated, he used to keep his arms so wide apart that we used to see his armpits." (Al-Bukhāriy no. 390, Muslim no. 495).

Besides, *Maymoonah*, may Allāh be pleased with her, narrated, "When the Prophet prostrated, he would make the space between his arms and sides such that it would allow a sheep to get through." (Muslim no. 496). This indicates that it is Sunnah to exaggerate in positioning the arms wide apart, provided this would not cause any harm to those praying next to one another, similar to what was mentioned about spreading the elbows away from the body in *Rukoo'*.

It is also Sunnah to keep the thighs away from each other when prostrating. *Abu Humayd* narrated, "He kept his thighs wide and did not let his belly touch his thighs." (Abū Dāwood no. 735)

It is agreed upon by all Scholars that this is Sunnah as reported by Imām Ash-Shawkāniy and others.

Ash-Shawkāniy, may Allāh have mercy on him, said, "This Hadeeth indicates that it is permissible to widen the space between the thighs during prostration, keeping them a distance away from the belly, and this is agreed on between the Scholars." (Nayl Al-Awttār, 2/547)

Timed Sunan

2. Ensuring the toes point towards the Qiblah while prostrating.

Abu Humayd reported, "I am the one who is most knowledgeable about the Prophet's ﷺ prayer." *Abu Humayd* then said in the same Hadeeth, "When he wanted to prostrate, he would place his hands on the ground neither stretching them nor grasping them and he would place his toes pointing towards the Qiblah." (Al-Bukhāriy no. 828)

As for the position of the fingers during prostration, it is Sunnah to keep them extended straight, tight together, and pointed towards the Qiblah.

It was reported in *Al-Muwatta'* by Imām Mālik that *'Abdallāh Ibn 'Umar*, may Allāh be pleased with them, said, "It is Sunnah to extend the palms of the hands straight, tighten between the fingers, and place the palms of the hands on the ground, with the fingers pointing towards the Qiblah." (Mussannaf of Ibn Abi Shaybah, 1/236)

3. Saying the Adthkār of Sunnah in prostration.

The following are some of the Adthkār of Sunnah that can be uttered after the obligatory supplication of prostration {سبحان ربي الأعلى} "Glory to my Lord the most High.":

1> « سُبْحَانَكَ اللَّهُمَّ رَبَّنَا وَبِحَمْدِكَ، اللَّهُمَّ اغْفِرْ لِي »

"Glory and praise be to You, O Allāh our Lord, I ask You your forgiveness." This is taken from the Hadeeth of *'Ā'ishah*, may Allāh be pleased with her. (Al-Bukhāriy no. 794, Muslim no. 484)

2> « سُبُّوحٌ قُدُّوسٌ رَبُّ الْمَلَائِكَةِ وَالرُّوحِ »

All-Glorious, All-Holy, Lord of the angels and spirit.". This supplication was narrated in the Hadeeth of *'Ā'ishah*, may Allāh be pleased with her. (Muslim no. 487)

3> « اللَّهُمَّ لَكَ سَجَدْتُ، وَبِكَ آمَنْتُ، وَلَكَ أَسْلَمْتُ، سَجَدَ وَجْهِي لِلَّذِي خَلَقَهُ وَصَوَّرَهُ، وَشَقَّ سَمْعَهُ وَبَصَرَهُ، تَبَارَكَ اللهُ أَحْسَنُ الْخَالِقِينَ »

"O Allāh, to You I prostrated, in You I believe, and to You I submit. My face prostrates to the One Who created it and gave it hearing and sight. Glory be to Allāh, the Best of creators." This supplication is narrated in the Hadeeth of *'Aliy* . (Muslim no. 771)

4) « اللَّهُمَّ اغْفِرْ لِي ذَنْبِي كُلَّهُ دِقَّهُ وَجِلَّهُ، وَأَوَّلَهُ وَآخِرَهُ، وَعَلَانِيَتَهُ وَسِرَّهُ »

"O Allāh, forgive all of my sins, those that were small and those that were big, and those done in public and those done in secret."

This supplication was narrated in the Hadeeth of *Abi Hurayrah* . (Muslim no. 483)

5) «اللَّهُمَّ أَعُوذُ بِرِضَاكَ مِنْ سَخَطِكَ، وَبِمُعَافَاتِكَ مِنْ عُقُوبَتِكَ، وَأَعُوذُ بِكَ مِنْكَ، لَا أُحْصِي ثَنَاءً عَلَيْكَ، أَنْتَ كَمَا أَثْنَيْتَ عَلَى نَفْسِكَ»

"O Allāh, I seek Your pleasure to guard us against Your anger, and Your mercy to guard us against Your punishment. I seek Your refuge against Your discontent. Whatever we do to praise You, we cannot praise You as You deserve. Praise be to you as much as You have praised Yourself." This supplication was reported in the Hadeeth of *'Ā'ishah*, may Allāh be pleased with her.

It is recommended to occasionally alternate between these formulae.

As for the obligatory supplications of both bowing {سبحان ربي العظيم} "Glory be to my Lord the Great," and prostration {سبحان ربي الأعلى} "Glory be to my Lord the most High," uttering them once is obligatory, and uttering them more than once up to three times is Sunnah.

4) Supplicating thoroughly in prostration.

This is because a worshiper in prostration is in closest position to his Lord, and thus it is Sunnah to instesify supplication in prostration, as mentioned in the Hadeeth reported by Muslim and narrated by *Ibn 'Abbāss*, may Allāh be pleased with them both, that the Prophet ﷺ said, "When you prostrate, strive hard in supplication, as this is when it is more likely to be answered." (Muslim no. 479)

Timed Sunan

⟨6⟩ **Sitting between the two prostrations.**

① Placing the left foot flat on the ground and sitting on it, and placing the right foot erect upright.

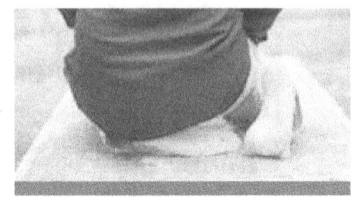

This is supported by the Saheeh (trusted) Hadeeth of *Abi Humayd Is-Sā'idiy* which states, "When the Prophet ﷺ sat between the two prostrations, he sat on his left foot and erected his right foot upright." (Al-Bukhāriy no. 828)

② Prolonging this pillar.

This is supported by the Hadeeth of *Thābit Il-Banāniy* that we have already mentioned.

③ Briefly sitting for rest before rising up to the second and fourth *Rak'ahs*.

It is Sunnah for one who is praying to sit for a while before he rises up to the second and fourth *Rak'ahs*, in an identical form to that of sitting between the two prostrations.

Note: This is a different action in prayer than that of sitting between the two prostrations, but it is mentioned here as it is identical in form to it.

It is called "Sitting for Rest", and it has no specific supplication. The legality of it has been proven in three different Ahādeeth, one of which is:

Mālik Ubn Ul-Huwayrith ؓ said, "I saw the Prophet ﷺ praying, and at the end of the odd *Rak'ahs* of his prayer he would not stand up until he sat down for a moment before rising to stand up." (Al-Bukhāriy no. 823)

Mālik Ubn Ul-Huwayrith ؓ is the same narrator who reported the Hadeeth of the Prophet ﷺ saying, "Pray like you have seen me praying." (Al-Bukhāriy no. 631)

The opinions of scholars varied regarding whether "Sitting for Rest" is Sunnah. The correct choice is that it is Sunnah as indicated by the Hadeeth of *Mālik* ؓ. Among the scholars who said that it is Sunnah are: *An-Nawawiy, Ash-Sawkāniy, Ibn Bāz, Al-Albāniy*, may Allāh have mercy on them all, and the *Permanent Committee for Scientific Research and Iftā'*.

An-Nawawiy, may Allāh have mercy on him, said, "This is the correct opinion as proven by the authentic Ahādeeth."

⟨7⟩ **Sunan of Tashahhud.**

Tashahhud is a position in prayer in which the worshiper sits down after the second *Rak'ah*, and after the last *Rak'ah* of prayer, and supplicates with a specific formula referred to as the supplication of Tashahhud.

Prayers consisting of two *Rak'ahs* have one Tashahhud at the end of the prayer, and prayers consisting of either three or four *Rak'ahs* have two Tashahhuds, one after the second *Rak'ah*, and the other after the last *Rak'ah* before the end of the prayer.

① In the position of sitting for Tashahhud, it is Sunnah to place the left foot flat on the ground and sit on it, and place the right foot erect upright.

This way of sitting should be followed in the position of Tashahhud after the second *Rak'ah* of any prayer, whether a two, three or four *Rak'ahs* prayer. *Abu Humayd Is-Sā'idiy* narrated in a Saheeh Hadeeth, "And when he sat after the second *Rak'ah*, he sat on his left foot and placed his right foot erect upright." (Al-Bukhāriy no. 828)

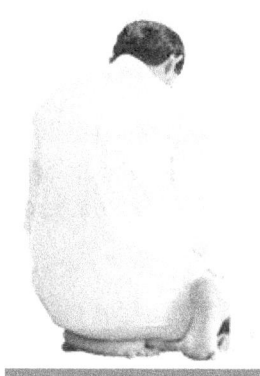

In addition, *'Ā'ishah*, may Allāh be pleased with her, narrated, "He used to say Tashahhud every two *Rak'ahs*, and he used to sit on his left foot and place his right foot erect upright." (Muslim no. 498)

As for the Tashahhud at the end of prayers comprising of three or four *Rak'ahs*, this will be presented later on.

Timed Sunan

② Occasionally alternating between the forms of Sunnah regarding the position of the hands during Tashahhud.

Positioning the hands during Tashahhud has two different forms:

Firstly, Placing the two hands on the thighs.

Secondly, Placing the two hands on the knees, with the left hand placed directly on top of the left knee, and the right fist pointing with the index finger as will be explained later on.

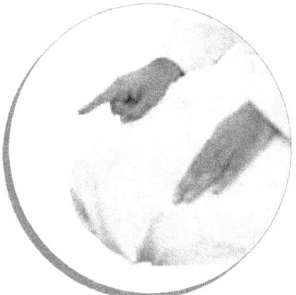

Ibn 'Umar, may Allāh be pleased with them, narrated, "When the Messenger of Allāh ﷺ used to sit for Tashahhud, he used to place his right hand on his right thigh, close his right fist tight, and point with his right index finger, and place his left hand on his left thigh." (Muslim no. 580) In another narration it says, "He loaded his left palm on his left knee." (Muslim no. 579)

③ Occasionally alternating between the forms of Sunnah regarding the position of the fingers during Tashahhud.

Positioning the fingers during Tashahhud has two different forms:

Firstly, To close the right fist, and point with the right index finger, while the fingers of his left hand are extended straight.

This is narrated in the Hadeeth of *Ibn 'Umar* ﷺ mentioned earlier in which he said, " … He would place his right hand on his right thigh, close his right fist tight, point with his right index finger, and place his left hand on his left thigh." (Muslim no. 580)

Secondly, To gesture with his right hand indicating number fifty-three. This is done by closing the little and ring fingers tight, touching the thumb with middle finger to make a ring shape, and pointing with the index finger. As for the left hand, the fingers are to be extended straight.

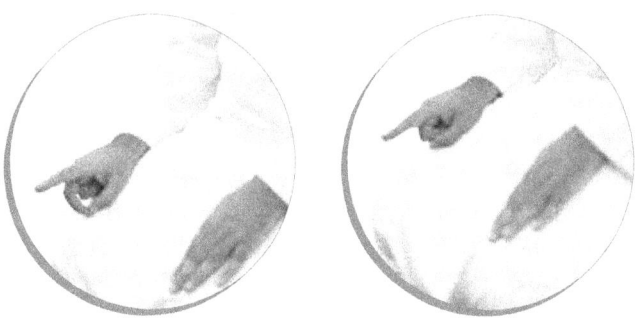

This is indicated in another narration of the Hadeeth of *Ibn 'Umar*, may Allāh be pleased with them both, saying, "When the Messenger of Allāh ﷺ used to sit for Tashahhud, he would place his left hand on his left knee, his right hand on his right knee, gesture with the fingers of his right hand to indicate number fifty-three, and point with the right index finger." (Muslim no. 580)

4 Occasionally alternating between of the different formulae of Sunnah of Tashahhud.

These different formulae include:

1) « التَّحِيَّاتُ لِلَّهِ، وَالصَّلَوَاتُ، وَالطَّيِّبَاتُ، السَّلَامُ عَلَيْكَ أَيُّهَا النَّبِيُّ وَرَحْمَةُ اللَّهِ وَبَرَكَاتُهُ، السَّلَامُ عَلَيْنَا وَعَلَى عِبَادِ اللَّهِ الصَّالِحِينَ، أَشْهَدُ أَنْ لَا إِلَهَ إِلَّا اللَّهُ، وَأَشْهَدُ أَنَّ مُحَمَّدًا عَبْدُهُ وَرَسُولُهُ »

"All compliments, prayers and pleasant things are due to Allāh. Peace be upon you, O Prophet, and Allāh's mercy and blessings be upon you. Peace be on us and on the true pious slaves of Allāh. I testify that none has the right to be worshiped but Allāh and that Muhammad is His slave and Messenger." (Al-Bukhāriy no. 1202, Muslim no. 402)

 « التَّحِيَّاتُ الْمُبَارَكَاتُ، الصَّلَوَاتُ الطَّيِّبَاتُ لِلَّهِ، السَّلَامُ عَلَيْكَ أَيُّهَا النَّبِيُّ... »

"All blessed compliments and sincere prayers are due to Allāh. Peace be on you, O Prophet, ..." then he would complete to the end as in the above formula. (Muslim no. 403)

Timed Sunan

3› « التَّحِيَّاتُ الطَّيِّبَاتُ الصَّلَوَاتُ لله ، السَّلامُ عَلَيْكَ أَيُّهَا النَّبِيُّ... »

"All pleasant compliments and prayers are due to Allāh. Peace be on you, O Prophet, ..." then he would complete to the end as in the above formula. (Muslim no. 404)

5› **Sitting in the form of Tawarruk in the last Tashahhud of prayers comprising of three or four *Rak'ahs*.**

In other words, the worshiper should sit on his left hip. Tawarruk was reported in different forms, and it is recommended to occasionally alternate between these forms.

Among these forms are the following:

1› To sit while spreading the left leg to the right side below the right leg, erecting the right foot in an upright position, with the buttocks resting on the ground.

This description is reported by Al-Bukhāriy through *Abi Humayd Is-Sā'idiy*. (Al-Bukhāriy no. 828)

2› To sit while spreading both legs to the right side, and letting the buttocks rest on the ground.

This description is reported by Abi Dāwood no. 731, Ibn Hibban no. 1867, and Al-Bayhaqiy 2/128 through *Abi Humayd Is-Sā'idiy*, and was authenticated by Imām Il-Albāniy, may Allāh have mercy upon them all.

It is however to be noted that according to the preponderant opinion, these positions are not relevant to every last Tashahhud, but they only relate to the last Tashahhud in prayers consisting of three or four *Rak'ahs*, not prayers consisting of two *Rak'ahs*.

Timed Sunan

6 Occasionally alternating between the different formulae of Sunnah of the supplications of sending peace and blessings upon Prophet Muhammad ﷺ.

Several formulae have been narrated for the supplications of sending peace and blessings upon Prophet Muhammad ﷺ in Tashahhud. It is Sunnah to occasionally alternate between these formulae, some of which are:

1) « اللَّهُمَّ صَلِّ عَلَى مُحَمَّدٍ، وَعَلَى آلِ مُحَمَّدٍ، كَمَا صَلَّيْتَ عَلَى إِبْرَاهِيمَ، وَعَلَى آلِ إِبْرَاهِيمَ إِنَّكَ حَمِيدٌ مَجِيدٌ، اللَّهُمَّ بَارِكْ عَلَى مُحَمَّدٍ، وَعَلَى آلِ مُحَمَّدٍ، كَمَا بَارَكْتَ عَلَى إِبْرَاهِيمَ وَعَلَى آلِ إِبْرَاهِيمَ إِنَّكَ حَمِيدٌ مَجِيدٌ »

"O Allāh, send Your Mercy on Muhammad and on the family of Muhammad, as You sent Your Mercy on Ibrāheem and on the family of Ibrāheem, for You are the Most Praiseworthy, the Most Glorious. O Allāh, send Your Blessings on Muhammad and on the family of Muhammad, as You sent Your Blessings on Ibrāheem and on the family of Ibrāheem, for You are the Most Praiseworthy, the Most Glorious." (Al-Bukhāriy no. 3370)

2) « اللَّهُمَّ صَلِّ عَلَى مُحَمَّدٍ وَعَلَى آلِ مُحَمَّدٍ كَمَا صَلَّيْتَ عَلَى آلِ إِبْرَاهِيمَ، وَبَارِكْ عَلَى مُحَمَّدٍ وَعَلَى آلِ مُحَمَّدٍ كَمَا بَارَكْتَ عَلَى آلِ إِبْرَاهِيمَ، فِي الْعَالَمِينَ، إِنَّكَ حَمِيدٌ مَجِيدٌ »

"O Allāh, send Your Mercy on Muhammad and on the family of Muhammad, as You sent Your Mercy on the family of Ibrāheem, and send Your Blessings on Muhammad and on the family of Muhammad, as You sent your Blessings on the family of Ibrāheem, for You are the Most Praiseworthy, the Most Glorious."

3) « اللَّهُمَّ صَلِّ عَلَى مُحَمَّدٍ وَعَلَى أَزْوَاجِهِ وَذُرِّيَّتِهِ، كَمَا صَلَّيْتَ عَلَى آلِ إِبْرَاهِيمَ، وَبَارِكْ عَلَى مُحَمَّدٍ وَعَلَى أَزْوَاجِهِ وَذُرِّيَّتِهِ، كَمَا بَارَكْتَ عَلَى آلِ إِبْرَاهِيمَ، إِنَّكَ حَمِيدٌ مَجِيدٌ »

"O Allāh, send Your Mercy on Muhammad and on his wives and offspring, as You sent Your Mercy on the family of Ibrāheem, and send Your Blessings on Muhammad and on his wives and offspring, as You sent Your Blessings on the family of Ibrāheem, for You are the Most Praise-worthy, the Most Glorious." (Al-Bukhāriy no. 3369, Muslim no. 407)

7 Seeking Allāh's refuge against four things before making Tasleem (Salutation, the last action in prayer).

This is the opinion of the scholars, may Allāh have mercy on them, supported by the Hadeeth narrated by *Abi Hurayrah* ﷺ that the Prophet ﷺ said, "When

Timed Sunan

any one of you completes the last Tashahhud, let him seek refuge in Allāh from four things: From the torment of Hell, from the torment of the grave, from the trials of life and death, and from the evil of Al-Maseeh Id-Dajjāl (Antichrist)." (Al-Bukhāriy no. 832, Muslim no. 588)

Besides, there are other supplications of Sunnah, and it is Sunnah for the worshiper to occasionally alternate between these supplications:

1> « اللَّهُمَّ إِنِّي أَعُوذُ بِكَ مِنَ الْمَأْثَمِ وَالْمَغْرَمِ »

"O Allāh, I seek refuge with You from sins and debt." (Al-Bukhāriy no. 832, Muslim no. 589)

2> « اللَّهُمَّ إِنِّي أَسْأَلُكَ الْجَنَّةَ وَأَعُوذُ بِكَ مِنَ النَّارِ »

"O Allāh, I ask You paradise and I seek refuge in you from Hellfire." (Abū Dāwood no. 792)

3> « اللَّهُمَّ إِنِّي ظَلَمْتُ نَفْسِي ظُلْمًا كَثِيرًا وَلَا يَغْفِرُ الذُّنُوبَ إِلَّا أَنْتَ، فَاغْفِرْ لِي مَغْفِرَةً مِنْ عِنْدِكَ وَارْحَمْنِي، إِنَّكَ أَنْتَ الْغَفُورُ الرَّحِيمُ »

"O Allāh, I have transgressed against myself and confess my sins, and no one forgives sins but You, so forgive my sins and have mercy on me for You are the Most Forgiving, the Most Merciful." (Al-Bukhāriy no. 6326, Muslim no. 2705)

4> « اللَّهُمَّ أَعِنِّي عَلَى ذِكْرِكَ، وَشُكْرِكَ، وَحُسْنِ عِبَادَتِكَ »

"O Allāh, assist me to remember You, to be thankful to You, and to worship You in the best manner." (Ahmad no. 22119, Abū Dāwood no. 1522 and An-Nasā'iy no. 1304)

5> « اللَّهُمَّ إِنِّي أَعُوذُ بِكَ مِنَ الْبُخْلِ، وَأَعُوذُ بِكَ مِنَ الْجُبْنِ، وَأَعُوذُ بِكَ أَنْ أُرَدَّ إِلَى أَرْذَلِ الْعُمُرِ، وَأَعُوذُ بِكَ مِنْ فِتْنَةِ الدُّنْيَا، وَأَعُوذُ بِكَ مِنْ عَذَابِ الْقَبْرِ »

"O Allāh, I seek refuge in You from miserliness, from cowardice, from senility, from the trial of life, and from the torment of the grave." (Al-Bukhāriy no. 6370)

6> « اللَّهُمَّ حَاسِبْنِي حِسَابًا يَسِيرًا »

"O Allāh, make my reckoning on the Day of Judgment easy." (Ahmad no. 24215)

Timed Sunan

He would then make Tasleem, turning his head to the right while saying {السلام عليكم ورحمة الله} then doing the same to the left. This act of turning the head to the right and left is Sunnah. Moreover, exaggeration in turning the head to the right and left during Tasleem is another Sunnah, as the Prophet ﷺ used to exaggerate in it that people behind him could see the whiteness of his cheeks. *Sa'd Ubn Abi Waqqāss* ؓ narrated, "I used to see Allāh's Messenger ﷺ making Tasleem to his right and left sides until I could see the whiteness of his cheeks." (Muslim no. 582)

⟨8⟩ **Supplications of Sunnah after obligatory prayers.**

By this we mean immediately after Tasleem from obligatory prayers.

Al-Imām Un-Nawawiy, may Allāh have mercy on him, said, "Scholars unanimously recommended the Adthkār after prayer." (Al-Adthkār, p.66)

It is recommended to raise one's voice while saying the supplications after prayer, as the Hadeeth of *Ibn 'Abbāss*, may Allāh be pleased with them, stated, "Raising one's voice in Adthkār after completing the obligatory prayers was practiced during the time of the Prophet ﷺ." (Al-Bukhāriy no. 841, Muslim no. 583)

Adthkār after obligatory prayers:

1⟩ Asking for forgiveness three times and then saying,

« اللَّهُمَّ أَنْتَ السَّلَامُ وَمِنْكَ السَّلَامُ، تَبَارَكْتَ ذَا الْجَلَالِ وَالْإِكْرَامِ »

"O Allāh, You are The Peace, and from You comes Peace. Blessed are You, O Owner of Majesty and Honor." (Muslim no. 591)

2⟩ « لَا إِلَهَ إِلَّا اللهُ وَحْدَهُ لَا شَرِيكَ لَهُ، لَهُ الْمُلْكُ وَلَهُ الْحَمْدُ وَهُوَ عَلَى كُلِّ شَيْءٍ قَدِيرٌ، لَا حَوْلَ وَلَا قُوَّةَ إِلَّا بِاللهِ، لَا إِلَهَ إِلَّا اللهُ، وَلَا نَعْبُدُ إِلَّا إِيَّاهُ، لَهُ النِّعْمَةُ وَلَهُ الْفَضْلُ، وَلَهُ الثَّنَاءُ الْحَسَنُ، لَا إِلَهَ إِلَّا اللهُ مُخْلِصِينَ لَهُ الدِّينَ، وَلَوْ كَرِهَ الْكَافِرُونَ »

"There is no God but Allāh alone, with no partner or associate. His is the kingdom and His is the praise, and He has power over everything. There is no power nor strength except with Allāh. There is no God but Allāh. We worship no one but Him alone. He owns all blessings, excellence, and the best of praise. There is no God but Allāh, to Whom we devote our sincere religion, even if the disbelievers dislike it." (Muslim no. 596)

Timed Sunan

3> « لَا إِلَهَ إِلَّا اللهُ وَحْدَهُ لَا شَرِيكَ لَهُ، لَهُ الْمُلْكُ وَلَهُ الْحَمْدُ وَهُوَ عَلَى كُلِّ شَيْءٍ قَدِيرٌ، اللَّهُمَّ لَا مَانِعَ لِمَا أَعْطَيْتَ، وَلَا مُعْطِيَ لِمَا مَنَعْتَ، وَلَا يَنْفَعُ ذَا الْجَدِّ مِنْكَ الْجَدُّ »

"There is no God but Allāh alone with no partner or associate. His is the kingdom and his is the praise, and He has power over everything. O Allāh, none can prevent what You have willed to bestow, and none can give what You hold back, and hard efforts by anyone for anything cannot benefit one against Your will." (Al-Bukhāriy no. 844, Muslim no. 593)

4> Then, it is Sunnah is to praise Allāh using one of the following formulae:

First: « سبحان الله » ثلاثا وثلاثين مرَّة ، و«الحمد لله» ثلاثا وثلاثين مرَّة،و«الله أكبر» ثلاثا وثلاثين مرَّة، وتمام المائة : « لا إله إلا الله وحده لا شريك له، له الملك وله الحمد وهو على كل شيء قدير »

"Subhān Allāh," (Glory be to Allāh) **thirty three times**, "Al-Hamdu Lillāh," (Praise be to Allāh) **thirty three times**, "Allāhu Akbar," (Allāh is the Greatest) **thirty three times**, and then completing the hundred with "Lā Ilāha Illā Allāh Wahdahu Lā Shareeka Lah, Lahu Al-Mulku Wa Lahu Al-Hamdu Wa Huwa 'Ala Kulli Shay'in Qadeer," (There is no God but Allāh alone with no partner or associate. His is the kingdom and his is the praise, and He has power over everything).

Abu Hurayrah ﷺ reported that the Prophet ﷺ said,

«مَنْ سَبَّحَ اللهَ فِي دُبُرِ كُلِّ صَلَاةٍ ثَلَاثًا وَثَلَاثِينَ، وَحَمِدَ اللهَ ثَلَاثًا وَثَلَاثِينَ، وَكَبَّرَ اللهَ ثَلَاثًا وَثَلَاثِينَ، فَتِلْكَ تِسْعَةٌ وَتِسْعُونَ، وَقَالَ تَمَامَ الْمِائَةِ: لَا إِلَهَ إِلَّا اللهُ وَحْدَهُ لَا شَرِيكَ لَهُ، لَهُ الْمُلْكُ وَلَهُ الْحَمْدُ وَهُوَ عَلَى كُلِّ شَيْءٍ قَدِيرٌ، غُفِرَتْ خَطَايَاهُ وَإِنْ كَانَتْ مِثْلَ زَبَدِ الْبَحْرِ»

"He who says after every prayer, 'Subhān Allāh,' (Glory be to Allāh) **thirty three times**, 'Al-Hamdu Lillāh,' (Praise be to Allāh) **thirty three times**, 'Allāhu Akbar,' (Allāh is the Greatest) **thirty three times**, and completes the hundred with, 'Lā Ilāha Illā Allāh Wahdahū Lā Sharika Lah, Lahu Al-Mulku Wa Lahu Al-Hamdu Wa Huwa *'Ala* Kulli *Shay'in* Qadeer,' (There is no God but Allāh alone with no partner or associate. His is the kingdom and His is the praise and He has power over everything), will have all his sins forgiven even if they were as abundant as the foam on the surface of the sea." (Muslim no. 597)

Timed Sunan

Second: «سبحان الله» ثلاثا وثلاثين مرَّة، و«الحمد لله» ثلاثا وثلاثين مرَّة، و«الله أكبر» أربعا وثلاثين مرَّة

"Subhān Allāh," (Glory be to Allāh) **thirty three times**, "Al-Hamdu Lillāh," (Praise be to Allāh) **thirty three times**, "Allāhu Akbar," (Allāh is the Greatest) **thirty four times**.

Ka'b Ubn 'Ujrah narrated that the Prophet said, "There are some statements after every obligatory prayer the performers of which will never be caused disappointment; making Tasbeeh (saying "Subhān Allāh.") **thirty three times**, making Tahmeed (saying "Al-Hamdu Lillāh.") **thirty three times**, and making Takbeer (saying "Allāhu Akbar.") **thirty four times**." (Muslim no. 596)

Third: «سبحان الله» خمسا وعشرين مرَّة، و«الحمد لله» خمسا وعشرين مرَّة، و«الله أكبر» خمسا وعشرين مرَّة، و«لا إله إلا الله» خمسا وعشرين مرَّة

"Glory be to Allāh," **twenty five times**, "Praise be to Allāh," **twenty five times**, "Allāh is the Greatest," **twenty five times**, and "There is no God but Allāh," **twenty five times**.

This formula was reported by At-Tirmidthiy through *'Abdillāh Ibn Zayd*. (At-Tirmidthiy no. 3413)

Fourth: «سبحان الله» عشر مرات، و«الحمد الله» عشر مرات، و«الله أكبر» عشر مرات

"Glory be to Allāh," **ten times**, "Praise be to Allāh," **ten times**, and "Allāh is the Greatest," **ten times**.

These formulae were reported in the Hadeeth of *'Abdillāh Ibn 'Amr*, may Allāh be pleased with them both. (At-Tirmidthiy no. 3410)

As stated earlier, the rule regarding acts of worship or supplications that were reported in different forms or formulae, is that it is Sunnah to occasionally alternate between these forms or formulae.

It is Sunnah to use the fingers for counting when making Tasbeeh. Both Ahmad and At-Tirmidthiy reported that the Prophet said, "Count Tasbeeh using your fingers, for verily they will be questioned and made to speak." (Ahmad no. 27089, At-Tirmidthiy no. 3486)

Fifth: Reciting Āyat Al-Kursiy (The Verse of the Throne):

Abu Umāmah narrated that Allāh's Messenger said, "Whoever recites Āyat Al-Kursiy after every obligatory prayer, nothing is between him and Paradise but death." (Sunan *An-Nasā'iy* Al-Kubra no. 9928)

 Timed Sunan

Sixth: Reciting *Al-Mu'awidthatayn* (i.e. *Soorat Il-Falaq* no. 113, and *Soorat In-Nās* no. 114)

'Uqbah Ubn 'Āmir ﷺ narrated, "The Messenger of Allāh ﷺ commanded me to read the *Mu'awwidthatayn* after every prayer." (Abū Dāwood no. 1525).

These were different types of Sunan that are recommended to be applied by the Muslim. Yet we are still proceeding with the topic of "Sunan of Fajr Time". We mentioned these Sunan, however, as they are related to Fajr prayer as well as all other prayers, and Allāh knows best.

⟨9⟩ **Remaining seated after finishing Fajr prayer in one's place of prayer until the sun rises.**

Jābir Ubn Samurah ﷺ narrated, "The Prophet ﷺ used to remain seated in his place in the mosque after praying Fajr until the sun fully rises." (Muslim no. 670)

◆ Prophet Muhammad, may Allāh's peace and blessings be upon him, said, "Allāh will shade seven (types of people) on the day when there will be no other shade but His; and he mentioned from among them, a man whose heart is very much attached to mosques."

Timed Sunan

Adthkār of the Morning

Time for Adthkār of the Morning starts from the time of Fajr (i.e. once the *Mu'adthin* makes Adthān). Undoubtedly, Adthkār are protection for the Muslim in this life, and treasures of reward in the Hereafter.

Adthkār of the Morning (and the Evening):

1. "Whoever says,

« لَا إِلَهَ إِلَّا اللَّهُ وَحْدَهُ لَا شَرِيكَ لَهُ، لَهُ الْمُلْكُ وَلَهُ الْحَمْدُ، وَهُوَ عَلَى كُلِّ شَيْءٍ قَدِيرٌ »

'There is no God but Allāh alone, with no partner or associate. His is the kingdom and His is the Praise, and He has power over everything,' **ten times in the morning**, a hundred good deeds will be written for him, a hundred bad deeds will be erased from his record, he will get reward equivalent to that of freeing a slave, and he will have protection on that day until the evening comes, and whoever says this supplication **ten times in the evening**, he will get the same reward until the morning comes." (Ahmad no. 8719, and Shaykh Ibn Bāz graded its Isnād as Hassan [Good])

Timed Sunan

2 ﴿ أَمْسَيْنَا وَأَمْسَى الْمُلْكُ للهِ، وَالْحَمْدُ للهِ لَا إِلَهَ إِلَّا اللهُ وَحْدَهُ لَا شَرِيكَ لَهُ اللَّهُمَّ إِنِّي أَسْأَلُكَ مِنْ خَيْرِ هَذِهِ اللَّيْلَةِ وَخَيْرِ مَا فِيهَا، وَأَعُوذُ بِكَ مِنْ شَرِّهَا وَشَرِّ مَا فِيهَا، اللَّهُمَّ إِنِّي أَعُوذُ بِكَ مِنَ الْكَسَلِ، وَالْهَرَمِ، وَسُوءِ الْكِبَرِ، وَفِتْنَةِ الدُّنْيَا، وَعَذَابِ الْقَبْرِ ﴾

"We have entered upon evening, while the whole kingdom is for Allāh, and praise is due to Allāh alone Whom there is no God but Him and has no partner or associate. O Allāh, I ask You from the good of this night and the good of what it contains, and I seek refuge in You from the evil of this night and the evil of what it contains. O Allāh, I seek refuge in You from laziness, senility, and the evil of vanity, and I seek refuge in You from the trial of this life, and from the torment of the grave."

In the morning he used to say,

﴿ أَصْبَحْنَا وَأَصْبَحَ الْمُلْكُ للهِ ... أَسْأَلُكَ خَيْرَ مَا فِي هَذَا الْيَومِ وَخَيْرَ مَا بعده، وَأَعُوذُ بِكَ مِنْ شَرِّ مَا فِي هَذَا الْيَومِ وَشَرِّ مَا بَعْدَهُ ﴾

"We entered upon morning, while the whole kingdom is for Allāh, and praise is due to Allāh alone Whom there is no God but Him and has no partner or associate. O Allāh, I ask You from the good of this day and the good of what comes after it, and I seek refuge in You from the evil of this day and what comes after it ..." (Muslim no. 2723)

3 *Sayyid Ul-Istighfār* (The master supplication of asking forgiveness):

﴿ اللَّهُمَّ أَنْتَ رَبِّي لَا إِلَهَ إِلَّا أَنْتَ خَلَقْتَنِي، وَأَنَا عَبْدُكَ، وَأَنَا عَلَى عَهْدِكَ وَوَعْدِكَ مَا اسْتَطَعْتُ، أَعُوذُ بِكَ مِنْ شَرِّ مَا صَنَعْتُ، أَبُوءُ لَكَ بِنِعْمَتِكَ عَلَيَّ، وَأَبُوءُ لَكَ بِذَنْبِي فَاغْفِرْ لِي فَإِنَّهُ لَا يَغْفِرُ الذُّنُوبَ إِلَّا أَنْتَ ﴾

"O Allāh, You are my Lord. None has the right to be worshiped but You. You have created me and I am Your slave, and I am faithful to my covenant with you and my promise to you as much as I can. I seek refuge in You from all the evil I have done. I acknowledge before You all the blessings You have bestowed upon me, and I confess to You all my sins, so forgive my sins, for nobody can forgive sins except You."

The Prophet ﷺ said, "Whoever says this supplication during the day with firm faith in it and dies on the same day before the evening, he will be from the people of Paradise, and whoever says it at night with firm faith in it, and dies before the morning, he will be from the people of Paradise." (Al-Bukhāriy no. 6306)

Timed Sunan

4 The Prophet ﷺ said, "When the morning comes say,

«اللَّهُمَّ بِكَ أَصْبَحْنَا، وَبِكَ أَمْسَيْنَا، وَبِكَ نَحْيَا، وَبِكَ نَمُوتُ، وَإِلَيْكَ النُّشُورُ»

"O Allāh, by You we enter the morning and by You we enter the evening, by You we live, and by You we die, and to You is the final return," and when the evening comes say,

«اللَّهُمَّ بِكَ أَمْسَيْنَا، وَبِكَ أَصْبَحْنَا، وَبِكَ نَحْيَا وَبِكَ، نَمُوتُ، وَإِلَيْكَ المَصِيرُ»

"O Allāh, by You we enter the evening and by You we enter the morning, by You we live and by You we die, and to You is the resurrection."
(Abū Dāwood no. 5068, At-Tirmidthiy no. 3391, Sunan *An-Nasā'iy* Al-Kubra no. 9836 and Ibn Mājah no. 3868, and Shaykh Ibn Bāz graded its Isnād as Saheeh [Authentic])

5 «اللَّهُمَّ فَاطِرَ السَّمَوَاتِ وَالْأَرْضِ، عَالِمَ الْغَيْبِ وَالشَّهَادَةِ، لَا إِلَهَ إِلَّا أَنْتَ رَبَّ كُلِّ شَيْءٍ وَمَلِيكَهُ، أَعُوذُ بِكَ مِنْ شَرِّ نَفْسِي وَمِنْ شَرِّ الشَّيْطَانِ وَشَرَكِهِ، وَأَنْ أَقْتَرِفَ عَلَى نَفْسِي سُوءًا، أَوْ أَجُرَّهُ إِلَى مُسْلِمٍ»

"O Allāh, Creator of the heavens and the earth, Knower of the unseen and the evident, Lord and Possessor of everything, I bear witness that there is none worthy of worship but You. I seek refuge in You from the evil of my soul and from the evil of Satan and his encouragement to associate others with you, and from bringing evil on myself or bringing evil to another Muslim."

Allāh's Messenger said,

"Say it in the morning, in the evening, and when you go to bed." (Ahmad no. 6597, Abū Dāwood no. 3529, and *An-Nasā'iy* no. 7699, and Shaykh Ibn Bāz graded its Isnād as Saheeh [Authentic])

6 «بِسْمِ اللَّهِ الَّذِي لَا يَضُرُّ مَعَ اسْمِهِ شَيْءٌ فِي الْأَرْضِ وَلَا فِي السَّمَاءِ وَهُوَ السَّمِيعُ الْعَلِيمُ»

"In the Name of Allāh, with Whose Name there is protection against every kind of harm in the earth or in the heaven, and He is the All-Hearing and the All-Knowing"

The Prophet ﷺ said, "Whoever says, 'In the Name of Allāh, with Whose Name there is protection against every kind of harm in the earth or in the heaven, and He is the All-Hearing and the All-Knowing,' **three times in the morning** and **three times in the evening**, nothing will harm him."(Ahmad no. 446, At-Tirmidthiy no. 10179 and Ibn Mājah no. 3869, and graded as Hassan Saheeh [Good-Authentic] by At-Tirmidthiy and Ibn Bāz)

Timed Sunan

7

« رَضِيتُ بِاللهِ رَبًّا، وَبِالْإِسْلَامِ دِينًا، وَبِمُحَمَّدٍ صَلَّى اللهُ عَلَيْهِ وَسَلَّمَ نَبِيًّا، إِلَّا كَانَ حَقًّا عَلَى اللهِ أَنْ يُرْضِيَهُ يَوْمَ الْقِيَامَةِ »

"I am pleased with Allāh as my Lord, with Islam as my religion, and with Muhammad ﷺ as my Prophet."

The Prophet ﷺ said, "No Muslim slave of Allāh would say **three times in the morning** and **three times in the evening**, 'I am pleased with Allāh as my Lord, with Islam as my religion, and with Muhammad ﷺ as my Prophet,' but is promised by Allāh please him on the day of resurrection." (Ahmad no. 18967, At-Tirmidthiy no. 3389, and Ibn Mājah no. 3870, and Shaykh Ibn Bāz graded its Isnād as Hassan [Good])

8

« اللَّهُمَّ إِنِّي أَسْأَلُكَ الْعَافِيَةَ فِي الدُّنْيَا وَالْآخِرَةِ، اللَّهُمَّ إِنِّي أَسْأَلُكَ الْعَفْوَ وَالْعَافِيَةَ فِي دِينِي وَدُنْيَايَ، وَأَهْلِي وَمَالِي، اللَّهُمَّ اسْتُرْ عَوْرَاتِي، وَآمِنْ رَوْعَاتِي، اللَّهُمَّ احْفَظْنِي مِنْ بَيْنِ يَدَيَّ وَمِنْ خَلْفِي، وَعَنْ يَمِينِي وَعَنْ شِمَالِي، وَمِنْ فَوْقِي، وَأَعُوذُ بِعَظَمَتِكَ أَنْ أُغْتَالَ مِنْ تَحْتِي »

"O Allāh, I ask you for well-being in this world and in the Hereafter. O Allāh, I ask You for well-being in my religious and worldly affairs, and my family and my property. O Allāh, conceal my faults, calm my fears, and protect me from before me and behind me, from my right and my left, and from above me, and I seek refuge in Your Might from being taken unaware from beneath me." (Ahmad no. 4785, Abū Dāwood no. 5074, Sunan *An-Nasā'iy Al-Kubra* no. 10401, and Ibn Mājah no. 3871)

9

« أَعُوذُ بِكَلِمَاتِ اللهِ التَّامَّاتِ مِنْ شَرِّ مَا خَلَقَ »

"I seek refuge in the perfect words of Allāh from the evil of what He has created." (Ahmad no. 7898 and At-Tirmidthiy no. 3437. Narrated by *Abi Hurayrah* ﷺ, and Ibn Bāz graded its Isnād as Hassan [Good])

10

« أَصْبَحْنَا عَلَى فِطْرَةِ الْإِسْلَامِ، وَكَلِمَةِ الْإِخْلَاصِ، وَدِينِ نَبِيِّنَا مُحَمَّدٍ صَلَّى اللهُ عَلَيْهِ وَسَلَّمَ، وَمِلَّةِ أَبِينَا إِبْرَاهِيمَ حَنِيفًا مُسْلِمًا، وَمَا كَانَ مِنَ الْمُشْرِكِينَ »

"We have entered a new day upon the religion of Islam, the word of sincere devotion, the religion of our Prophet Muhammad ﷺ, and the faith of our father Ibrāheem who was an upright Muslim (in worshiping Allāh), and was not of those who worship others besides Allāh." (Ahmad no. 21144, 15367)

When the night comes he would say,

"We have entered a new night upon the religion of Islam… etc."

Ibn Bāz graded the Isnād of this Hadeeth as Saheeh [Authentic].

All the supplications mentioned above are collected in a book by Shaykh Ibn Bāz, may Allāh have mercy on him, entitled "Tuhfat Ul-Akhyār Bi Bayān Jumlah *Nafi'ah* Mimma Warada Fee Il-Kitābi Wa As-Sunnah Mina *Al-Ad'iyah Wa Al-Adthkār*," in the chapter of "Adthkār of the Day and the Night".

⑪ « يَا حَيُّ يَا قَيُّومُ بِرَحْمَتِكَ أَسْتَغِيثُ أَصْلِحْ لِي شَأْنِي كُلَّهُ، وَلَا تَكِلْنِي إِلَى نَفْسِي طَرْفَةَ عَيْنٍ »

"O Ever Living One, O Sustainer, by Your Mercy I seek relief. Set right for me all my affairs. Do not place me in charge of myself, even for the blinking of an eye (i.e. even for a moment)." (*An-Nasā'iy* in Al-Sunan Al-Kubra no. 10405)

⑫ « حَسْبِيَ اللهُ لاَ إِلَهَ إِلاَّ هُوَ عَلَيْهِ تَوَكَّلْتُ وَهُوَ رَبُّ الْعَرْشِ الْعَظِيمِ »

"Sufficient for me is Allāh, there is no God worthy of worship except Him, on Him I have relied, and He is the Lord of the Great Throne," **seven times in the morning** and **seven times in the evening**. (Abū Dāwood no. 5081)

 Timed Sunan

Dhuhā Time

It is Sunnah for a Muslim at the time of Dhuhā (forenoon) to offer Dhuhā prayer.

This is proven by the following Ahādeeth:

1. The Hadeeth of *Abi Hurayrah* ﷺ, who said, "My beloved one (i.e. the Prophet ﷺ) advised me to do three things: To fast three days in every month, to offer the two *Rak'ah* prayer of Ad-Dhuhā, and to offer Witr prayer before sleeping." (Authenticated by Al-Albāniy)

   The Prophet ﷺ also advised *Aba d-Dardā'* ﷺ to offer the two *Rak'ahs* of Dhuhā. (Muslim no. 722)

   Moreover, the Prophet ﷺ also advised *Abā Dtharr* ﷺ to offer the two *Rak'ahs* of Dhuhā. (*An-Nasā'iy* in As-Sunan Al-Kubrā no. 2712)

2. The Hadeeth of *Abi Dtharr* ﷺ, who reported that the Prophet ﷺ said, "By every morning, every one of you owes to give Sadaqah (charity) on behalf of every joint of his bones. Every Tasbeehah (saying "Subhān Allāh" [Glory be to Allāh]) is a charity, every Tahmeedah (saying

"Al-Hamdu Lillāh" [All praise and thanks be to Allāh]) is a charity, every Tahleelah (saying "Lā Ilāha Illā Allāh" [None has the right to be worshiped except Allāh]) is a charity, every Takbeerah (saying "Allāhu Akbar" [Allāh is Greater]) is a charity, enjoining the good is a charity, and forbidding the evil is a charity. However, a sufficient substitute for all of this is to offer two *Rak'ahs* at the time of Dhuhā." (Muslim no. 720)

It was also reported in Saheeh Muslim by *'Ā'ishah*, may Allāh be pleased with her, that every person was created with three hundred and sixty joints, and he who does an equivalent number of acts of Sadaqah (charity), will walk on that day (i.e. the day of judgment) having distanced himself from Hellfire. (Muslim, no. 1007)

The time for Dhuhā prayer:

Its time begins when the sun has risen above the horizon by the height of a spear (i.e. when the time of prohibition is over).

The time for Dhuhā prayer ends just before midday (i.e. about ten minutes before the time for Dthuhr prayer).

This is proven by the Hadeeth of *'Amr Ibn 'Absah*, to whom the Prophet said, "Offer the morning prayer, then refrain from praying when the sun rises until it has risen high, for when it rises, it rises between the two horns of a devil and at that time the disbelievers prostrate to it. Then pray, for prayer is witnessed and attended until the shadow of a vertical spear covers no more than the spear itself (i.e. when the sun is directly overhead at midday). Then refrain from praying, for at that time Hellfire is stoked up." (Muslim no. 832)

The preferred time for Dhuhā prayer is by the end of the prescribed time, which is when the young weaned camels feel the severity of the sun's heat.

This is proven by the Hadeeth of *Zayd Ibn Arqam*, who stated the Prophet said, "The prayer of Al-Awwabeen is when the young weaned camels feel the severity of the sun's heat." (Muslim no. 748)

Shaykh Ibn Bāz, may Allāh have mercy on him, said, "The Arabic word [Tarmadh] used in the Hadeeth means that the heat of the sun becomes severe on them, while the word [Al-Fissāl] refers to the young offspring of camels. Thus, Dhuhā is a prayer the performance of which is preferable by the end of the permitted time." (Fatāwā Islāmiyyah 1/515)

 Timed Sunan

The number of *Rak'ahs* of Dhuhā prayer:

The least is two *Rak'ahs*. This is proven by the Hadeeth of *Abi Hurayrah* ﷺ, who said, "My beloved one (i.e. the Prophet ﷺ) advised me to do three things: To fast three days in every month, to offer the two *Rak'ahs* of Dhuhā, and to offer Witr prayer before sleeping." (Al-Bukhāriy no. 1981, Muslim no. 721)

As for the upper limit of the number of *Rak'ahs* of Dhuhā prayer, there actually is no upper limit for those who want to pray more than two *Rak'ahs*. Some scholars said that the upper limit is eight *Rak'ahs*, but this is not a strong choice. In fact, a Muslim is allowed to exceed eight *Rak'ahs* to whatever number of *Rak'ahs* he would like to pray, as proven by the Hadeeth of *'Ā'ishah*, may Allāh be pleased with her, who said, "The Prophet used to pray Dhuhā four *Rak'ahs*, and then he would go beyond that by whatever number of additional *Rak'ahs* that Allāh willed." (Muslim no. 719)

◆ This is the advice of the Prophet, may Allāh's peace and blessings be upon him, to his companions due to the virtues of Dhuhā prayer (forenoon voluntary prayer).

Fourth: Dthuhr Time (Noon)

The regular Sunnah before and after Dthuhr prayer:

We have already discussed the regular Sunan, and we mentioned that it is of the regular Sunan to offer four *Rak'ahs* before Dthuhr prayer and two *Rak'ahs* after Dthuhr prayer, as indicated by the Hadeeth of *'Ā'ishah, Umm Habeebah*, and *Ibn 'Umar*, may Allāh be pleased with them all.

Prolonging the first *Rak'ah* of Dthuhr prayer:

This is proven by the Hadeeth of *Abi Sa'eed Il-Khudriy* ﷺ, who said: "The Iqāmah for Dthuhr prayer would be made, and any one of us would go to *Al-Baqee'*, relieve himself, perform ablution and come back to the mosque, and the Messenger of Allāh ﷺ would still be in the first *Rak'ah*, prolonging it." (Muslim no. 454)

 Timed Sunan

Thus, it is Sunnah to prolong the first *Rak'ah* of Dthuhr prayer. The same is applicable when a person prays alone, and also for a woman when she prays Dthuhr. Unfortunately, this practice is one of the neglected Sunan, may Allāh, the Almighty, make us of those who are eager to apply the Sunnah and adhere to it.

 Delaying Dthuhr prayer when it is very hot, until it cools down:

This is proven by the following Hadeeth:

Abu Hurayrah narrated that the Prophet said, "If it is very hot, then pray Dthuhr prayer when it becomes cooler, as the severity of the heat is from the rage of Hellfire." (Al-Bukhāriy no. 533-534, Muslim no. 615)

Shaykh Ubn 'Uthaymeen, may Allāh have mercy on him, said, "Thus, if we say that Zawāl in summer is at 12:00 p.m. and *'Asr* is at 4:30 p.m., this means that the time of Ibrād (cooling down) may be valid until nearly 4:00 p.m." (*Al-Mumti'* 2/104).

Ibrād is general, for one who is praying in congregation, and for one who is praying alone. This is the correct opinion that was adopted by *Shaykh Ibn 'Uthaymeen*, may Allāh have mercy on him. This includes women too, because the Hadeeth of *Abi Hurayrah* is general and did not specify a gender.

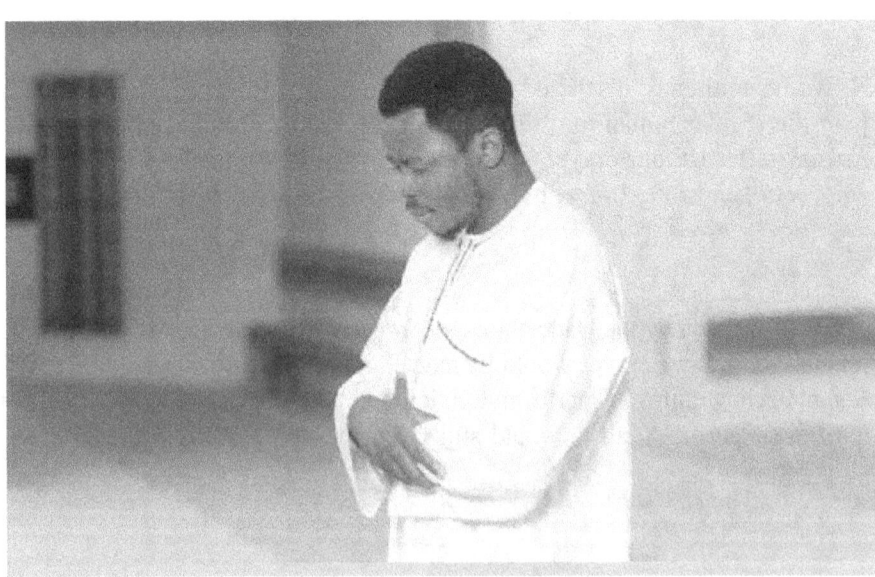

◆ Prophet Muhammad, may Allah's peace and blessings be upon him, said, "...and prayer is light. Have mercy to light the lives in this life, and the Hereafter."

Timed Sunan

Fifth: 'Asr Time

 There is no regular Sunnah before 'Asr prayer.

We have already discussed the regular Sunan in detail, and we mentioned that there are no regular Sunan to be performed before *'Asr* prayer.

Shaykh Ul-Islam Ibn Taymiyyah, may Allāh have mercy on him, said, "None of the scholars said that the Prophet ﷺ used to perform any regular Sunnah before *'Asr* prayer. What was reported in this regard is either weak or even incorrect." (Al-Fatāwā, 23/125)

Thus, the correct opinion, and Allāh knows best, is that no certain Sunnah is specified before *'Asr* prayer, but it is rather left unrestricted. Hence, if someone wants to pray two *Rak'ahs* or more before *'Asr* as a general Nāfilah that is not specifically intended to be a regular Sunnah before *'Asr* prayer, he can do so as he would do at any other time that is not a time of prohibition. In conclusion, it is not allowed to offer a Sunnah prayer before *'Asr* prayer with the intention that it is specific to being before *'Asr*.

The time for Adthkār of the Evening (and the Morning):

Question:

When does the time for Adthkār of the morning and the evening start?

Answer:

The time for Adthkār of the Evening:

It appears, and Allāh knows best, that the correct opinion is that the time for Adthkār of the Evening starts after *'Asr* prayer and continues until sunset (Maghrib). Moreover, it is also allowed to perform Adthkār of the Evening after Maghrib, especially for someone who had an excuse to delay them until after Maghrib.

The time for Adthkār of the Morning:

The time for Adthkār of the Morning starts at the break of the true dawn, namely the time for Fajr prayer. Thus, the time for morning Adthkār begins when the *Mu'adthin* makes Adthān for Fajr. This is the opinion of the majority of scholars, may Allāh have mercy on them all.

Timed Sunan

Sixth: Maghrib Time

 Preventing children from playing outside at this time.

 Locking the doors at the beginning of Maghrib time and mentioning Allāh's name.

Applying these two acts of Sunnah protects from the evil of devils and Jinn. Preventing children from playing outside particularly at this time will protect them against devils. In addition, locking the doors and mentioning Allāh's name will keep devils away. This shows the great attention of Islam to protecting homes and kids from evil.

Timed Sunan

This is proven by the following Hadeeth:

Jābir Ubn 'Abdillāh narrated that Allāh's Messenger said, "When night falls keep your children indoors, for the devils spread out at that time. When an hour of the night elapses, you can let them go. Close the doors and mention the Name of Allāh, for Satan does not open a closed door." (Al-Bukhāriy no. 3304, Muslim no. 2012)

However, it should be noted that keeping children indoors and closing the doors is just a recommended Sunnah, not an obligation. (Fatāwā of the Permanent Committee, 26/317)

◆ Praying two *Rak'ahs* before Maghrib prayer.

'Abdullāh Ibn Mughaffal Il-Muzaniy narrated that the Prophet said, "Offer a prayer before Maghrib prayer," and he said in the third time of his command, "... for any one who wishes," so that people would not take it as a regular or assured Sunnah. (Al-Bukhāriy no. 1183)

It is also Sunnah to pray two *Rak'ahs* between the Adthān and the Iqāmah of any of the daily obligatory prayers:

Praying any two *Rak'ahs* of Sunnah would suffice for these two *Rak'ahs*. This includes any two *Rak'ahs* of regular Sunnah that can be performed at this time, such as the two *Rak'ahs* of regular Sunnah before Fajr or Dthuhr. On the other hand, if a person is sitting in the mosque and for example the Adthān of 'Asr or 'Ishā' is performed, and there is no specific regular Sunnah to be performed, it is still Sunnah to stand up and offer two *Rak'ahs* of Sunnah between Adthān and Iqāmah.

This is proven by the following Hadeeth:

'Abdullāh Ibn Mughaffal Al-Muzaniy narrated that the Prophet said,

"There is a prayer between every two Adthāns (Adthān and Iqāmah)," he said it three times and he added, "... for any one who wishes." (Al-Bukhāriy no. 624, Muslim no. 838)

Timed Sunan

There is no doubt that the two *Rak'ahs* before Maghrib or between Adthān and Iqāmah are not assured Sunan like the regular Sunan are, but they can rather be left sometimes. It is for this reason that the Prophet ﷺ said, "… for any one who wishes," to make sure that people do not consider them as a regular or assured Sunnah.

 It is disliked to sleep before *'Ishā'* prayer.

Abu Barzah Al-Aslamiy narrated, "The Prophet ﷺ used to favor delaying *'Ishā'* prayer, and he used to dislike sleeping before it and talking after it."
(Al-Bukhāriy no. 599, Muslim no. 647)

The reason why sleeping before *'Ishā'* prayer is disliked is that it is feared that one might oversleep, and this may cause him to miss *'Ishā'* prayer.

◆ Repentance during the day and night is the key for one to rectify his pathway towards Allāh, the Exalted. Prophet Muhammad, may Allāh's peace and blessings be upon him, said, "Allāh, the Almighty, extends His Hand at night for the sinner of day to repent, and extends His Hand in the day for the sinner of night to repent."

Timed Sunan

Seventh: *'Ishā'* Time

> Talking and gatherings are disliked after *'Ishā'* prayer.

This is proven by the previous Hadeeth of *Abi Barzah Al-Aslamiy* in which he said, "... and the Prophet used to dislike sleeping before it and talking after it."

Note: If talking after *'Ishā'* is required for some need, then it is not disliked.

The reason that it is disliked to stay awake after *'Ishā'*, and Allāh knows best, is that one might oversleep and miss Fajr prayer, or miss night prayer if it was his habit to do so.

> It is preferred to delay *'Ishā'* prayer, provided no harm is caused by this delay to the followers of the Imām.

 **Timed Sunan**

This is proven by the following Hadeeth:

Ā'ishah, may Allāh be pleased with her, narrated, "The Prophet ﷺ stayed awake for a while one night until most of the night was gone and worshipers in the mosque fell asleep due to this delay. The Prophet ﷺ then came out and prayed, and then he said, 'It is its time now, had it not been difficult for my nation.'." (Muslim no. 638)

Thus, it is Sunnah for a woman, as she is not entitled to follow the congregational prayer, to delay *'Ishā'* prayer if this would not cause her any harm. The same applies to a man if he is in a situation in which he is not entitled to congregational prayer due to any relevant reason such as travel or otherwise.

 It is Sunnah to recite *Soorat Al-Ikhlās* (Chapter 112) every night.

Abu d-Dardā' ﷺ reported that the Prophet ﷺ said, "Is it difficult for any one of you to recite one third of the *Qur'ān* in one night?" They said, "How could one recite one third of the *Qur'ān* (in one night)?" He replied, "{Say: He is Allāh, the One,} (i.e. *Soorat Ul-Ikhlās*) is equal to one third of the *Qur'ān*." (Al-Bukhāriy and Muslim)

Timed Sunan

Sunan of Sleep

 Locking the doors when going to sleep.

Jābir Ibn 'Abdillāh narrated that the Prophet said, "Turn off any lamps when you go to bed, shut the doors, and cover containers of water and food." (Al-Bukhāriy no. 5624, Muslim no. 2012)

The reason behind locking the doors is to prevent devils from entering as was mentioned in the previous Hadeeth narrated by Jābir Ibn 'Abdillāh, may Allāh be pleased him, that the Prophet said, "… and lock your doors and mention Allāh's name, as the devil does not open a locked door." (Al-Bukhāriy no. 5623, Muslim no. 2012)

 Extinguishing the fire before going to sleep.

This is taken from the previous Hadeeth of Jābir Ibn 'Abdillāh , in which he said, "Turn off the lamps when you go to bed."

In addition, *Ibn 'Umar* narrates that the Prophet said, "Do not leave the fire burning in your homes when you go to bed." (Muslim no. 2015)

Furthermore, anything that can be a reason for setting the house on fire is forbidden to be kept on during the night. Great caution should be taken regarding heaters, ovens, and anything that might set a house on fire. The Prophet informed us that fire is an enemy.

However, if the relevant precautions are taken, and the fire, heater, or oven is safe and would not cause any harm, then nothing would be wrong with keeping them on during the night if one wishes.

Timed Sunan

3 Making ablution before going to bed.

Al-Barā' Ubn 'Āzib narrated that the Prophet said, "When you want to go to bed, perform ablution as you do for prayer, then lie down on your right side and say, 'O Allāh, I submitted my face towards You ...'." (Al-Bukhāriy no. 247, Muslim no. 2710)

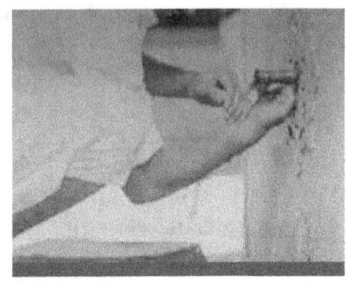

4 Dusting the bed off before going to sleep.

Abu Hurayrah narrated that the Prophet said, "When one of you goes to bed, he should dust his bed off with the inner side of his lower garment, for he does not know what came onto it after he left it. He should then say, 'In Your name, my Lord, I lie down, and in Your name I rise. If You take my soul then show mercy on it, and if You return it then protect it as You protect Your righteous slaves.'." (Al-Bukhāriy no. 6320, Muslim no. 2714)

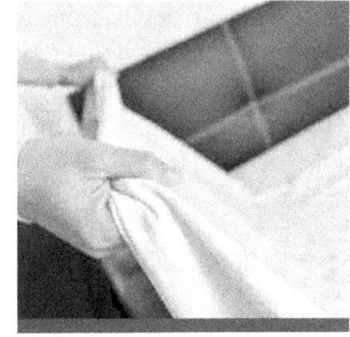

These Ahādeeth indicate that dusting off the bed is an act of Sunnah. Other authentic Ahādeeth indicate that dusting off the bed should be done three times, and Allāh's name should be mentioned while doing so.

It is recommended to dust the bed off with the inner side of the garment. Some scholars however, including *Shaykh Ibn Jibreen*, may Allāh have mercy upon him, said that anything can be used to dust the bed off, not necessarily the inner side of the garment. He said that this can be achieved even by using one's turban. (Fatwā no. 2693)

5 Lying on the right side.

6 Placing one's right hand under his right while lying down for sleep.

These two Sunan are proven by the following Ahādeeth:

Al-Barā' Ubn 'Āzib narrated that the Prophet said, "Upon going to bed, perform

Timed Sunan

ablution as you do for prayer, then lie down on your right side and say, 'O Allāh, I submitted my face towards You ...'." (Al-Bukhāriy no. 2710, Mulsim no. 247)

In addition, *Hudthayfah* narrated, "The Prophet would put his hand under his cheek when he lied down for sleep at night." (Al-Bukhāriy no. 6314)

7 Saying the Adthkār of going to sleep.

1 Adthkār of going to sleep, from the *Qur'ān*:

1> Reciting Āyat Il-Kursiy.

It is Sunnah to recite Āyat Il-Kursiy before sleeping, as it protects the Muslim from Satan until the morning.

Abu Hurayrah narrated, "... Then the Prophet asked me, 'What did your prisoner do last night?' I answered, 'He promised to teach me some words which he claimed will benefit me before Allāh, so I let him go.' The Prophet asked, 'What are those words that he taught you?' I said, 'He told me, "When you go to bed, recite Āyat Al-Kursiy from its beginning to its end. If you do so, a guardian will be appointed by Allāh to protect you during the night, and no devil will be able to approach you until the morning.' The Prophet said, 'Verily, he told you the truth although he is a liar. O *Abā Hurayrah*, do you know with whom you were speaking for the last three nights?' I said, 'No.' The Prophet replied, 'That was a devil.'." (Al-Bukhāriy no. 2311)

2> Reciting the last two verses of *Soorat Il-Baqarah*.

Abu Mas'ood Il-Ansāriy narrated that Allāh's Messenger said, "Whoever recites the last two verses of *Soorat Il-Baqarah* at night, they shall be sufficient for him." (Al-Bukhāriy no. 4008, Muslim no. 807)

Timed Sunan

Yet, these two verses are not of the Adthkār of sleep in particular, but they are rather from the Adthkār of the night. Thus, one who did not recite them at night can recite them when he goes to bed.

The opinions of scholars varied regarding the interpretation of the meaning of the phrase "shall be sufficient for him." Some scholars said that it means they will give him reward as if he performed voluntary night prayer (Qiyām Al-Layl). Other scholars said that it means that they will protect him against the devil. A third opinion says that it means they will protect him against anything that might harm him. *An-Nawawiy*, may Allāh have mercy on him, said they would bring about all of these virtues.

3> Reciting *Soorat Il-Ikhlās*, *Soorat Il-Falaq*, and *Soorat In-Nās*, blowing with their reitation into one's hands, then wiping the body with the hands three times.

This is proven by the following Hadeeth:

'Ā'ishah, may Allāh be pleased with her, said, "When the Messenger of Allāh ﷺ would go to bed every night, he would bring his hands together and blow in them, and he would recite in them *Soorat Al-Ikhlās*, *Soorat Al-Falaq*, and *Soorat An-Nās*, then he would wipe with them over whatever he is able to reach of his blessed body, starting at his head and face, then moving to the rest of his body. He would do this three times." (Al-Bukhāriy no. 5017)

The following could be learnt from the previous Hadeeth:

The Prophet ﷺ used to apply this Sunnah every night as *'Ā'ishah*, may Allāh be pleased with her, mentions, ".. every night," and one who wants to apply this Sunnah should do it the same way the Prophet ﷺ did.

4> Reciting *Soorat Il-Kāfiroon*.

'Urwah Ubn Nawfal narrated through his father that the Prophet ﷺ said to Nawfal, "Recite *Soorat Al-Kāfiroon* and let it be the last thing you recite before you sleep, for it clears you from Shirk (polytheism)." (Ahmad no. 21934, Abū Dāwood no. 5055 and At-Tirmidthiy no. 3403)

Timed Sunan

2 **Adthkār of going to sleep, from the Sunnah:**

There are many supplications in the Sunnah for going to sleep, some of which are:

1 « بِاسْمِكَ اللَّهُمَّ أَمُوتُ وَأَحْيَا »

"O Allāh by Your name I die and I revive." (Al-Bukhāriy no. 6324)

2 « اللَّهُمَّ خَلَقْتَ نَفْسِي وَأَنْتَ تَوَفَّاهَا، لَكَ مَمَاتُهَا وَمَحْيَاهَا، إِنْ أَحْيَيْتَهَا فَاحْفَظْهَا، وَإِنْ أَمَتَّهَا فَاغْفِرْ لَهَا، اللَّهُمَّ إِنِّي أَسْأَلُكَ الْعَافِيَةَ »

"O Allāh, You have created my soul and You take it back. Unto You is its death and its life. If You give it life then protect it, and if You cause it to die then forgive it. O Allāh, I ask You well-being." (Muslim no. 2712)

3 « اللَّهُمَّ رَبَّ السَّمَاوَاتِ وَرَبَّ الْأَرْضِ وَرَبَّ الْعَرْشِ الْعَظِيمِ، رَبَّنَا وَرَبَّ كُلِّ شَيْءٍ، فَالِقَ الْحَبِّ وَالنَّوَى، وَمُنْزِلَ التَّوْرَاةِ وَالْإِنْجِيلِ وَالْفُرْقَانِ، أَعُوذُ بِكَ مِنْ شَرِّ كُلِّ شَيْءٍ أَنْتَ آخِذٌ بِنَاصِيَتِهِ، اللَّهُمَّ أَنْتَ الْأَوَّلُ فَلَيْسَ قَبْلَكَ شَيْءٌ، وَأَنْتَ الْآخِرُ فَلَيْسَ بَعْدَكَ شَيْءٌ، وَأَنْتَ الظَّاهِرُ فَلَيْسَ فَوْقَكَ شَيْءٌ، وَأَنْتَ الْبَاطِنُ فَلَيْسَ دُونَكَ شَيْءٌ، اقْضِ عَنَّا الدَّيْنَ وَأَغْنِنَا مِنَ الْفَقْرِ »

"O Allāh, Lord of the seven heavens and Lord of the Magnificent Throne. Our Lord and the Lord of everything. Splitter of the grain and seeds, Revealer of the Torah and the Injeel and the Furqān (i.e. the Qur'ān), I seek refuge in You from every evil that You seize by the forelock. O Allāh, You are the First and nothing has come before you, and You are the Last and nothing may come after You. You are the Evident and nothing is above You, and You are the Innermost and nothing is beyond You. Remove our burdens of debt and enrich us against poverty." (Muslim no. 2713)

4 « بِاسْمِكَ رَبِّي وَضَعْتُ جَنْبِي وَبِكَ أَرْفَعُهُ، إِنْ أَمْسَكْتَ نَفْسِي فَارْحَمْهَا، وَإِنْ أَرْسَلْتَهَا فَاحْفَظْهَا بِمَا تَحْفَظُ بِهِ عِبَادَكَ الصَّالِحِينَ »

"With Your Name, my Lord, I laid myself down, and with Your Name I rise. If You take my soul show mercy on it, and if You send it back then protect it like You protect Your righteous slaves." (Al-Bukhāriy no. 6302, Muslim no. 2714)

'Ishā' Time

Timed Sunan

5> ﴿ الْحَمْدُ لِلَّهِ الَّذِي أَطْعَمَنَا وَسَقَانَا، وَكَفَانَا وَآوَانَا، فَكَمْ مِمَّنْ لاَ كَافِيَ لَهُ وَلاَ مُؤْوِي ﴾

Anass said, "Upon going to bed, Allāh's Messenger used to say, 'Praise be to Allāh who fed us, gave us drink, gave us what is sufficient for us, and gave us shelter. Many are those who have no one to provide sufficiency for them or give them shelter.'." (Mulsim no. 2715)

6> ﴿ اللَّهُمَّ قِنِي عَذَابَكَ يَوْمَ تَبْعَثُ عِبَادَكَ ﴾

"O Allāh, protect me against Your punishment on the day You resurrect Your slaves." (Ahmad no. 18660)

7> Glorifying Allāh (saying "Subhān Allāh") **thrity three times**, Praising Allāh (saying "Al-Hamdu Lillāh") **thrity three times**, and saying "Allāh is Greater" ("Allāhu Akbar") **thirty four times** when going to bed for sleep.

This has great virtue, and gives the body strength throughout the day.

This is proven by the following Hadeeth: *Aliy* narrated that *Fātimah*, may Allāh be pleased with her, went to the Prophet complaining about the effect of the stone hand-mill on her hands. She heard that the Prophet had received a few servants. When she came there she did not find him, so she mentioned her problem to *'Ā'ishah*. When the Prophet came, *'Ā'ishah* informed him about that. *'Aliy* added, "So the Prophet came to us when we had gone to bed. We wanted to get up on his arrival but he said, 'Stay where you are.' He then came and sat between me and her and I felt the coldness of his feet on my chest. He said, 'Shall I direct you to something better than what you have requested? When you go to bed say "Allāhu Akbar" thirty-four times, "Subhān Allāh" thirty-three times, and "Al-Hamdu Lillāh" thirty-three times, for that is far better for you than a servant.'." (Al-Bukhāriy no. 3705, Muslim no. 2727)

In another narration, *'Aliy* said, "I have never left them since I heard about them from the Prophet." He was asked, "Even on the night of the battle of Siffeen?" He said, "Even on the night of the battle of Siffeen." (Al-Bukhāriy no. 5362, Muslim no. 2727)

Timed Sunan

⟨ اللَّهُمَّ إِنِّي أَسْلَمْتُ وَجْهِي إِلَيْكَ، وَفَوَّضْتُ أَمْرِي إِلَيْكَ، وَأَلْجَأْتُ ظَهْرِي إِلَيْكَ، رَغْبَةً وَرَهْبَةً إِلَيْكَ. لَا مَلْجَأَ وَلَا مَنْجَا مِنْكَ إِلَّا إِلَيْكَ، آمَنْتُ بِكِتَابِكَ الَّذِي أَنْزَلْتَ، وَبِنَبِيِّكَ الَّذِي أَرْسَلْتَ ⟩ ⟨8⟩

"O Allāh, I submitted my face to You, entrusted my affairs to You, and relied completely on You, out of desire and fear of You. There is no resort or escape from You except with You. I believe in Your Book that You have revealed, and in Your Prophet whom You have sent."
(Al-Bukhāriy no. 247, Muslim no. 2710)

◆ Remembrance of Allāh is a well-fortified fortress and a cause for enlivening the heart, so be of those who constantly remember Allāh.
Prophet Muhammad, may Allāh's peace and blessings be upon him, said, "One who remembers his Lord compared to one who does not remember his Lord, is like the living compared to the dead."

Timed Sunan

In another Hadeeth, the Prophet ﷺ said, "... and make them of the last of what you utter before sleeping, so if you die during the night, you will have died while you are on the Fitrah (i.e. natural disposition)". In Muslim's narration it says, "... and if you wake up in the morning, you will have woken up on well-being."

In this Hadeeth there is another Sunnah, which is to ensure these words are the last words to be uttered before sleeping. This has a great reward if it was the person's fate to die during this night, for if one who performed this Sunnah dies during this night, he will be upon the Fitrah of Ibrāheem, and if he wakes up in the morning, he will wake up on well-being. Note that "well-being" is a general term that encompasses the previously mentioned rewards in addition to other sorts of reward, and Allāh knows best.

Finally, it is worth drawing the attention of the reader here that the Dthikr in the following Hadeeth is a great Dthikr that entails great reward that Allāh, the Almighty, has blessed us with:

سَيِّدُ الاسْتِغْفَارِ أَنْ يَقُولَ: « اللَّهُمَّ أَنْتَ رَبِّي لا إِلَهَ إِلا أَنْتَ خَلَقْتَنِي وَأَنَا عَبْدُكَ وَأَنَا عَلَى عَهْدِكَ وَوَعْدِكَ مَا اسْتَطَعْتُ أَعُوذُ بِكَ مِنْ شَرِّ مَا صَنَعْتُ أَبُوءُ لَكَ بِنِعْمَتِكَ عَلَيَّ وَأَبُوءُ بِذَنْبِي فَاغْفِرْ لِي إِنَّهُ لاَ يَغْفِرُ الذُّنُوبَ إِلاَّ أَنْتَ » قَالَ : وَمَنْ قَالَهَا مِنَ النَّهَارِ مُوقِنًا بِهَا فَمَاتَ مِنْ يَوْمِهِ قَبْلَ أَنْ يُمْسِيَ فَهُوَ مِنْ أَهْلِ الْجَنَّةِ ، وَمَنْ قَالَهَا مِنَ اللَّيْلِ وَهُوَ مُوقِنٌ بِهَا فَمَاتَ قَبْلَ أَنْ يُصْبِحَ فَهُوَ مِنْ أَهْلِ الْجَنَّةِ

Shaddād Ubn Awss narrated that the Prophet ﷺ said, "The most superior way of asking Allāh forgiveness is, 'O Allāh, you are my Lord. There is no God worthy of worship but You. You created me and I am Your servant, and I uphold Your covenant and my promise to You to the most of my ability. I seek refuge in You from the evil I have done. I acknowledge before You Your favor upon me, and I acknowledge my sin; so forgive me, as indeed, there is none who can forgive sins except You.'." The Prophet ﷺ added, "Whoever peforms this supplication in the morning with firm faith in it and dies on the same day will be from the people of Paradise, and whoever peforms it in the night with firm faith and dies during the same night will be from the people of Paradise."
(Al-Bukhāriy no. 6306)

◆ Sunan of Dreams:

According to the Hadeeth of *Abi Hurayrah*, a dream is one of three types:

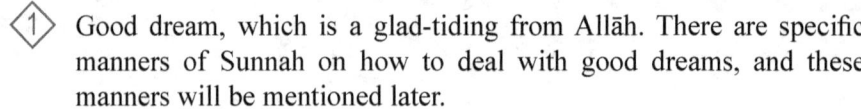
Good dream, which is a glad-tiding from Allāh. There are specific manners of Sunnah on how to deal with good dreams, and these manners will be mentioned later.

Timed Sunan

② bad dream, and it is from Satan. There are specific manners of Sunnah on how to deal with bad dreams. If these manners are followed, sad dreams will never cause any harm.

③ A person may dream about what he was thinking about before sleeping, and it is nothing to worry about.

◆ **The Ahādeeth that illustrate the Sunan of Dreams:**

Abu Salamah narrated, "I used to have dreams that would make me sick. I then heard *Abā Qatādah* saying, 'I used to have dreams that would make me sick, until I heard the Prophet saying, "A good dream is from Allāh, so if any one of you has a dream which he likes, he should not tell it to anybody except to someone whom he loves, and if he has a dream which he dislikes, then he should blow three times towards his left side, seek refuge with Allāh from from the evil of Satan and from the evil of this dream, and he should not tell it to anybody, and thus it will not harm him.".'."

Abu Salamah also said, "I used to have dreams the burden of which is heavier on me than the mountain of Uhud. Since I heard this Hadeeth however, I would just not care about them." (Al-Bukhāriy no. 5747, Muslim no. 2261)

In another narration, "A good dream is from Allāh, and a bad dream is from Satan, so if any one of you sees a dream that he fears, he should blow on his left side and seek refuge with Allāh from the evil of this dream, and thus it will not harm him." (Al-Bukhāriy no. 3292, Muslim no. 2261)

Jābir narrated that the Prophet said, "… and let him ask Allāh's refuge against Satan, and let him turn around and sleep on his other side." (Muslim no. 2262)

Abu Saʿeed Il-Khudriy narrated that the Prophet said, "If any one of you saw a dream which he liked then it is from Allāh, and thus he should praise Allāh for it." (Al-Bukhāriy no. 7045)

◆ **Summary of the acts of Sunnah to be done on seeing good/bad dreams:**

① **It is Sunnah for one who sees a good dream to do the following:**

Firstly: Praise Allāh, because it is from Him.

Secondly: Only tell it to those whom he loves.

 Timed Sunan

 On the other hand, it is Sunnah for one who sees a bad dream to do the following:

Firstly: Blow on his left side three times.

Secondly: Seek refuge in Allāh, the Almighty, from Satan and from the evil of what he saw by saying, "I seek refuge in Allāh from Satan and from the evil of this dream," three times.

Thirdly: Avoid telling it to anyone in order to avoid its harm as the Prophet ﷺ commanded.

Fourthly: Turn around and sleep on the other side. If one is sleeping on his back then he should turn to sleep on his side, and so on.

Fifthly: Rise up from sleep and pray two *Rak'ahs*.

We can conclude the following from the previous Ahādeeth:

A Muslim's dream is a part of the Prophecy, and thus if a Muslim is truthful while he is awake, his dreams will be closer to truth and reality. This is the effect and blessing of truthfulness on the life of a Muslim, even while sleeping.

 The Dthikr of Sunnah that one should utter upon waking up during the night:

'Ubādah Ubn Us-Sāmit ﷺ said that the Messenger of Allāh ﷺ said: "Whoever wakes up in the night and says:

« لَا إِلَهَ إِلَّا اللهُ وَحْدَهُ لَا شَرِيكَ لَهُ، لَهُ الْمُلْكُ وَلَهُ الْحَمْدُ وَهُوَ عَلَى كُلِّ شَيْءٍ قَدِيرٌ، الْحَمْدُ لِلَّهِ، وَسُبْحَانَ اللهِ، وَلَا إِلَهَ إِلَّا اللهُ، وَاللهُ أَكْبَرُ، وَلَا حَوْلَ وَلَا قُوَّةَ إِلَّا بِاللهِ »

'None has the right to be worshiped but Allāh. He is the only One and has no partners. His is the Kingdom and his is the Praise. He is Omnipotent. All Praise is for Allāh, all Glory is for Allāh, none has the right to be worshiped but Allāh, Allāh is Greater, and there is neither Might nor Power except with Allāh,' and then says, 'O Allāh, forgive me,' or asks Allāh, he will be responded to, and if he performs ablution and prays, his prayer will be accepted." (Al-Bukhāriy no. 1154)

Timed Sunan

There are two great glad-tidings mentioned in this Hadeeth. If a person wakes up and says this Dthikr, he will get two rewards:

If he says, "O Allāh forgive me," or makes *Du'ā'*, then his *Du'ā'* will be answered.

If he performs *Wudū'* and prays, his prayer will be accepted.

We have now concluded the section of Timed Sunan.

Praise be to Allāh who has bestowed us with these great rewards, and may Allāh assist us to do good.

Non-timed Sunan

This forms the second section of the daily Sunan, and this section is detailed and contains various Sunan, some of which change due to change of place, people, or time.

In this section, our effort is exerted to present the Sunan that are repetitively practiced during the day and night.
May Allāh grant us guidance and success.

Non-timed Sunan

First: Sunan of Eating

1 Saying "Bismillāh" (In the name of Allāh) before eating or drinking.

'Umar Ubn Abi Salamah narrated, "I was a boy under the care of Allāh's Messenger and my hand used to go around the dish while eating. Allāh's Messenger said to me, 'O boy, mention the Name of Allāh, eat with your right hand, and eat of the dish what is nearest to you.' Since then I have always applied these instructions while eating." (Al-Bukhāriy no. 5376, Mulsim no. 2022)

If a person forgets to mention Allāh's name at the beginning of eating, when he remembers he should say, "In the name of Allāh for its beginning and for its end."

'Ā'ishah, may Allāh be pleased with her, narrated that the Prophet said, "When one of you eats, he should mention Allāh's name (i.e. say Bismillāh). If he forgets to mention Allāh's Name at the beginning, when he remembers he should say, 'Bismillāhi Awwalahu wa Ākhirah' (In the name of Allāh for its beginning and for its end)." (Abū Dāwood no. 3767 and At-Tirmidthiy no. 1858)

This Hadeeth also indicates that a Muslim should eat using his right hand so he would not resemble Satan. Thus, if one did not say "Bismillāh", or ate with his left hand, he would resemble Satan.

This is proven by the following Hadeeth:

'Abdullāh Ibn 'Umar narrated that Allāh's Messenger said, "None of you should eat with his left hand, nor drink with it, for verily Satan eats with his left hand, and drinks with his left hand."

Nafi' added that the Prophet said, "… and none of you should take with the left hand, nor give with it." (Muslim no. 2020)

Moreover, satan is eager to enter homes so he can spend the night and share the food and drink of people.

Jābir Ubn 'Abdillāh narrated that he heard Allāh's Messenger saying, "When a man enters his house and mentions the Name of Allāh upon entering and upon eating, Satan says (addressing his followers), 'You will find nowhere to spend the night, and you will find no dinner,' but if he enters without mentioning the Name of Allāh upon entering, Satan says to his followers, 'You have found a place to spend the night, as well as dinner.'." (Muslim no. 2018)

  Eating from what is nearest to you of the dish.

This is proven by the Hadeeth of *'Umar Ubn Abi Salamah* mentioned earlier, narrating the advice given by the Prophet to the young boy saying, "… and eat from what is nearest to you of the dish." (Al-Bukhāriy no. 5376, Mulsim no. 2022)

  Picking up a piece of food that has fallen, cleaning it, then eating it.

Jābir Ubn 'Abdillāh narrated that he heard Allāh's Messenger saying, "Satan is present with every one of you in all of his matters, including when one of you eats, so when a piece of your food falls on the ground, pick it up, remove any of the dirt on it, and eat it in order not to leave it for Satan, and when you finish eating lick your fingers, for one of you does not know in which portion of the food the blessings lie." (Muslim no. 2033)

One who contemplates this Hadeeth will find Satan eager to share with man all of his affairs in order to spoil his life and make it void of blessings. What indicates this is the part of the previous Hadeeth that says, "Satan is present with every one of you in all of his matters …"

Non-timed Sunan

 Licking the fingers after eating.

This means to lick the thumb, index finger, and middle finger with the tip of your tongue, or have one's wife do so. In fact it is Sunnah to avoid wiping one's fingers with a tissue or cloth before licking them.

The previous Hadeeth of *Jābir Ibn 'Abdillāh* proves this.

Moreover, *Ibn 'Abbāss* narrated in the Saheehayn that the Prophet said, "When one of you finishes eating, he should not wipe his fingers until he has licked them or let someone else lick them." (Al-Bukhāriy no. 5456, Muslim no. 2033)

 Cleaning the dish.

This means to clean the dish by eating every piece or stain of food therein and not to leave anything. For example, when rice is served, every last grain of it should be eaten, as the blessings may lie in these remains. This applies in case it is not intended to keep the remaining food for later consumption.

What proves this is the following Hadeeth:

Anass reported, "The Prophet ordered us to clean the dish." (Muslim no. 2034)

In another narration by Muslim, "Every one of you should clean his dish." (Muslim no. 2035)

Shaykh Ubn 'Uthaymeen, may Allāh have mercy on him, said, "This means to take the little traces of food that stay behind with your fingers and lick them. Unfortunately, this is one of the Sunan that many people have abandoned, even some of the knowledge seeking students who are for sure aware of this Sunnah." (Sharh Riyādh Is-Sāliheen, 2/1069)

Non-timed Sunan

6. Eating with three fingers.

It is Sunnah to eat using three fingers; the thumb, the index finger, and the middle finger, especially with things that can be picked up easily with three fingers, like dates, etc.

This is proven by the following Hadeeth: *Ka'b Ubn Mālik* said, "The Prophet used to eat with three fingers, and he would lick them before wiping them." (Muslim no. 2032)

7. Taking three breaths outside the vessel during the course of drinking.

This means to drink in three gulps and breathe after each gulp.

This is proven by the following Hadeeth:

Anass said, "Allāh's Messenger used to breathe three times during the course of drinking, and used to say that drinking in this manner is more thirst quenching, healthier, and more relieving." *Anass* said, "Thus, I breathe three times during the course of drinking." (Al-Bukhāriy no. 5631, Muslim no. 2028)

The meaning here is that one should breathe outside the vessel, because breathing inside it is disliked as illustrated by *Abi Qatādah's* Hadeeth in the Saheehayn, in which Allāh's Messenger said, "When one of you drinks from a vessel, he should not breathe in it." (Al-Bukhāriy no. 5630, Muslim no. 267)

8. Thanking Allāh, the Almighty, after eating.

What proves this Sunnah is the following Hadeeth:

Anass narrated that the Prophet said, "Indeed, Allāh is pleased with His servant who when eats a morsel he praises Allāh for it, and when drinks a sip he praises Allāh for it." (Muslim no. 2743)

Non-timed Sunan

There are several formulae for praising Allāh, the Almighty, such as:

1. "All praise is due to Allāh; praise that is abundant, pure, and full of blessings. You feed your slaves and provide them, and You are not in need for anyone, nor can Your favors be abandoned or dispensed, O our Lord." (Al-Bukhāriy no. 5458)

2. "Praise be to Allāh our Lord, Who has satisfied our needs, and quenched our thirst. You feed your slaves and provide them, and You are not in need for anyone, nor can Your favors be denied, O our Lord." (Al-Bukhāriy no. 5459)

9 Gathering to have food.

It is Sunnah to gather for eating, and to avoid eating separately.

Abu Hurayrah narrated that Allāh's Messenger said, "The food of one person is sufficient for two people, and the food of two people is sufficient for four people, and the food of four people is sufficient for eight people." (Muslim no. 2059)

10 Praising the food if you like it.

It is Sunnah to praise the food if you like it, only with what is truly good about it.

Jābir Ubn 'Abdillāh narrated, "The Prophet asked for sauce and was told that there was nothing except vinegar. He then asked for it and began to eat from it, saying, 'What a good condiment vinegar is! What a good condiment vinegar is!'." (Muslim no. 2052) It should be noted that the vinegar they used was sweet, not sour like that we use today.

Shaykh Ubn 'Uthaymeen said, "It is from the Sunnah of the Prophet that if one likes food or bread, they should praise it. Moreover, it is also Sunnah to mention the name of the family that provided the food that one is praising." (Sharh Riyādh Is-Sāliheen 2/1057)

Non-timed Sunan

One who contemplates the reality nowadays will find that a lot of people not only do they not follow the Sunnah, but they even violate it by dishonoring and criticizing food in many situations. This is against the guidance of the Prophet ﷺ, as illustrated in the Hadeeth in the Saheehayn narrated by *Abi Hurayrah*, who said, "The Prophet ﷺ never criticized any food at all. If he liked it, he would eat it, and if he did not like it, he would leave it." (Al-Bukhāriy no. 3563, Muslim no. 2064)

 Making *Du'ā'* for the host.

Abdullāh Ibn Busr narrated, "Allāh's Messenger ﷺ came to my father and we served him a meal and a dish of dates, cheese, and butter. He ate from them, then he was given dates, which he would eat and place their stones between his fingers, and join his forefinger and middle finger. A drink was then brought to him and he drank it. He then gave it to the one who was on his right side." The narrator said, "My father took hold of the rein of the animal he used to ride and requested the Prophet ﷺ to supplicate for us. Thereupon he said, 'O Allāh, bless them in what You have provided them with as sustenance, forgive them, and have mercy upon them.'." (Muslim no. 2042)

 Offering water to others, starting first with the one on the right hand side.

After one drinks, it is Sunnah to pass on the vessel to someone on his right side.

Anass Ubn Mālik ؓ narrated, "Allāh's Messenger ﷺ came to our house and asked to drink, so we milked a sheep for him, and we mixed the milk with water from our well. I gave him the bowl, and he took it and drank from it. *Abu Bakr* was sitting on his left side, *'Umar* was in front of him, and a bedouin was on his right side. When the Prophet ﷺ finished drinking, Umar said to the Prophet, 'This is Abu Bakr', drawing the Prophet's attention to *Abi Bakr*. The Prophet however left out *Abā Bakr* and *'Umar*, and gave the remaining milk to the bedouin and said, 'Those on right! Those on right! Those on right!'." *Anass* ؓ added, "Thus it is Sunnah. Thus it is Sunnah. Thus it is Sunnah." (Al-Bukhāriy no. 2571, Muslim no. 2029)

Non-timed Sunan

13 One who serves water to the people should be the last one to drink.

Abu Qatādah said, "... The Prophet ﷺ then started pouring water for me and I would serve it to the people, until everyone drank except the Prophet ﷺ and I. The Prophet ﷺ then poured and said to me, 'Drink.' I said that I would not drink until he drank. He said, 'The one who serves water to the people should be the last to drink.' Thus, I drank and the Prophet ﷺ drank." (Mulsim no. 681)

It is Sunnah for one who drinks milk to rinse his mouth after finishing drinking so that no trace of fat will be left in his mouth. *Ibn 'Abbāss* narrated, "The Prophet ﷺ drank some milk and then asked for some water. He rinsed his mouth and said, 'It contains fat.'." (Al-Bukhāriy no. 211, Muslim no. 358)

14 Covering containers and mentioning the name of Allāh when the night comes.

It is Sunnah to cover any uncovered utensils or containers that have food or water in them when the night comes, and to mention Allāh's Name when doing so.

Jābir Ubn Abdillāh, may Allāh be pleased with them, narrated that he heard Allāh's Messenger ﷺ saying, "Cover utensils and tie up water skins, for there is one night in the year when pestilence descends, and it does not pass by any utensil that is not covered or any water skin that is not tied up, but some of this pestilence descends into it." (Muslim no. 2014)

In the narration of *Jābir Ibn Abdillāh* in Al-Bukhāriy, the Prophet ﷺ said, "Tie up your water skins and mention Allāh's Name, and cover your utensils and mention Allāh's Name, even if just by placing something over them." (Al-Bukhāriy no. 5623)

Non-timed Sunan

Second: Sunan of Greeting, Meeting, and Gathering

1. Greeting others with Salām (The greeting of peace).

There are numerous narrations that indicate this Sunnah.

Abu Hurayrah narrated that Allāh's Messenger said, "The duties of a Muslim towards other Muslims are six." The Prophet was asked, "Allāh's Messenger, what are these?" He answered, "When you meet him greet him, when he invites you accept his invitation, when he seeks your advice give him advice, when he sneezes and says, 'All praise is due to Allāh,' reply to him, 'Yarhamuk Allāh' (i.e. may Allāh's mercy be upon you), when he falls sick visit him, and when he dies follow his funeral." (Muslim no. 2162)

Replying to the greeting of Salām is obligatory.

Allāh, the Almighty, says, "And when you are greeted with a greeting, answer with a better greeting, or at least return it equally. Verily, Allāh keeps account indeed of all things." (*Soorat Un-Nisā'*)

Non-timed Sunan

An order from Allāh or the Prophet ﷺ originally means it is for obligation, unless another authentic proof proves otherwise.

Agreement of all scholars on the obligation of replying to a Muslim's greeting has been reported by several scholars, some of which are *Ibn Hazm, Ibn 'Abdil Barr, Shaykh Taqiy Ud-Deen*, and others, may Allāh have mercy on them.

The best formula of the greeting of Salām and response to it is, "May peace, the mercy of Allāh, and the blessings of Allāh be upon you."

Ibn Ul-Qayyim, may Allāh have mercy on him, said, "The Prophet's Sunnah when greeting someone is to complete this formula to the very end where it says, '... wa Barakātuh.' (i.e. and the blessings of Allāh be upon you)." (Zād Al-Ma'ād 2/417)

Spreading Salām among people is Sunnah. In fact it is an assured Sunnah that is greatly rewarded, as mentioned in the Hadeeth narrated by *Abi Hurayrah* ﷺ, that Allāh's Messenger ﷺ said, "By Him in whose Hand is my soul, you will not enter paradise until you believe, and you will not believe until you love one another. Shall I tell you about something you can do to love one another? Spread Salām among you." (Muslim no. 54)

 Repeating Salām three times if needed.

This is only valid in some cases, like when there is doubt whether the other person heard your greeting or not, in which case it is recommended to repeat it up to three times. Another example of this would be when there is a big gathering and only those in close vicinity hear the greeting, so repeating it is recommended up to three times in order to have all people hear.

This is proven by the following Hadeeth:

Anass ﷺ said, "When the Prophet ﷺ used to speak, he would repeat his words three times so people could understand him, and when he used to meet a group of people and greet them, he would greet them three times." (Al-Bukhāriy no. 95)

It can be concluded from the previous Hadeeth of *Anass* ﷺ, that it is Sunnah to repeat a word twice or thrice if needed, like in a situation where a person talks and he is not heard or understood.

Non-timed Sunan

3) Greeting those whom you know and those whom you do not know.

'Abdullāh Ibn 'Amr narrated, "A man asked the Messenger of Allāh, 'Which act in Islam is the best?' The Prophet replied, "To give food, and to greet those whom you know and those whom you do not know." (Al-Bukhāriy no. 12, Muslim no. 39)

4) Initiating Salām according to the rules that the Sunnah illustrated.

Abu Hurayrah narrated, "Allāh's Messenger said, 'One who is riding should greet one who is walking, one who is walking should greet one who is sitting, and the small group of people should greet the larger group of people.'." (Al-Bukhāriy no. 6233, Muslim no. 2160)

In another narration that Al-Bukhāriy reported, it says, "The young should greet the old, one who is walking should greet one who is sitting, and the small group of people should greet the large group of people." (Al-Bukhāriy no. 6234)

There is no problem, however, if someone does the opposite, like if the old greeted the young or if the one walking greeted the one riding, but it is of course better to follow the rules mentioned above as illustrated in the Sunnah.

5) Greeting children and shaking hands with them.

Anass Ubn Mālik narrated that he was walking with the Prophet and he passed by a group of children, and the Prophet greeted them. (Al-Bukhāriy no. 6247, Muslim no. 2168)

Greeting children and shaking hands with them shows humbleness, gets the children used to this, and raises the value of the Sunnah in their hearts.

6) Greeting those at home upon entering home.

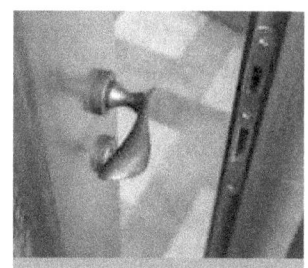

This falls under the general category of greeting others with Salām. It is Sunnah upon entering one's home to begin by cleaning his teeth with Siwāk (tooth-stick), and then to greet those at home with Salām.

 Non-timed Sunan

This is the fourth situation in which the use of Siwāk is recommended. *'Ā'ishah*, may Allāh be pleased with her, narrated, "The first thing that the Prophet ﷺ used to do upon entering home is using the Siwāk." (Muslim no. 253) Thus, he used to use the Siwāk first, and then greet his family members.

Some scholars even said that it is Sunnah to say the greeting of Salām upon entering any house, not just one's home, and that this should be done even if there was no one inside the house, as Allāh the Almighty says,

﴿ فَإِذَا دَخَلْتُم بُيُوتًا فَسَلِّمُوا عَلَىٰ أَنفُسِكُمْ تَحِيَّةً مِّنْ عِندِ اللَّهِ مُبَارَكَةً طَيِّبَةً كَذَٰلِكَ يُبَيِّنُ اللَّهُ لَكُمُ الْآيَاتِ لَعَلَّكُمْ تَعْقِلُونَ ﴾

"So when you enter houses, greet yourselves with Salām, a greeting from Allāh that is blessed and pure. This is how Allāh makes his revelations clear to you so perhaps you may understand." (*Soorat Un-Noor*, Verse 61)

Ibn Hajar, may Allāh have mercy on him, said, "This would be considered to fall under the general order to spread Salām. In a situation when one enters a place where no one exists, he should greet himself according to the instructions of *Qur'ān*ic verse mentioned above." (Fatth Ul-Bāri, Hadeeth 6235)

From the explanation above, **we can conclude that there are three Sunan upon entering home:**

1. To mention Allāh's name, especially at night. This is proven by the Hadeeth in which *Jābir Ubn 'Abdillāh*, may Allāh be pleased with them, narrated that he heard the Prophet ﷺ saying:

    "When a man enters his home and mentions the Name of Allāh upon entering and upon eating, Satan says (i.e. addressing his followers), 'You will find nowhere to spend the night and you will find no dinner,' but if he enters without mentioning the Name of Allāh, Satan says (to his followers), 'You have found a place to spend the night, as well as dinner.'." (Muslim no. 2018)

2. To use Siwāk, according to the Hadeeth of *'Ā'ishah*, may Allāh be pleased with her, that we already mentioned.

3. To greet the members of the family who are at home upon entering home.

Lowering one's voice when greeting people if some of them are asleep.

That was the practice of the Prophet ﷺ as mentioned in the narration of *Al-Miqdād Ibn Il-Aswad* who said, "… and we used to milk our animals and everyone would drink his share, and we would give the Prophet ﷺ his share, and he would come later and greet the people with a low voice that would not wake up someone asleep, but could be heard by those awake." (Muslim no. 2055)

 Conveying the greeting of Salām to others when asked by someone to do so.

Conveying Salām is Sunnah when asked by someone to convey Salām to someone else.

'Ā'ishah, may Allāh be pleased with her, narrated that the Prophet ﷺ said to her, "Jibreel conveys his Salām to you." She said, "Peace and mercy of Allāh be upon him." (Al-Bukhāriy no. 3217, Muslim no. 2447)

This Hadeeth indicates that one who is asked to convey greetings should convey them, like the Prophet conveyed the greeting of Jibreel to *'Ā'ishah*. Moreover, the Hadeeth also indicates that it is Sunnah to send greetings to others with someone.

 Greeting people with Salām upon arriving at a meeting, and upon leaving.

Abu Hurayrah narrated that Allāh's Messenger ﷺ said, "When one of you arrives at a meeting, he should give the greeting of Salām. Then when he leaves, he should also give the greeting of Salām. The former is no more of a duty than the latter." (Ahmad no. 9664, Abū Dāwood no. 5208 and At-Tirmidthiy no. 2706)

Non-timed Sunan

10 Shaking hands and greeting others with Salām upon meeting each other.

This was the practice of the companions who were very keen to follow the Sunnah.

Qatādah narrated. "I said to *Anass*, 'Was it the practice of the companions to shake hands with one another?' He said, 'Yes.'." (Al-Bukhāriy no. 6263)

11 Smiling.

Abu Dtharr narrated that Allāh's Messenger said to him, "Do not underestimate any good deed, even if it was just to meet your brother with a cheerful face." (Muslim no. 2626)

At-Tirmidthiy reported through *Abi Dtharr* that Allāh's Messenger said, "Smiling in the face of your brother is a charity." (At-Tirmidthiy no. 1956)

12 Using polite and decent words.

Using polite and decent words when meeting or sitting with someone is from the Sunnah, and is an act of charity.

Abu Hurayrah narrated that Allāh's Messenger said, "… and the pleasant word is a charity." (Al-Bukhāriy no. 2989, Muslim no. 1009)

Polite and decent words that people commonly use can be a means to obtain great reward, if just accompanied with the intention of doing charity.

Shaykh Ubn 'Uthaymeen, may Allāh have mercy on him, said, "Pleasant words are such as saying, 'How are you?', 'How are your brothers?', 'How is your family?', and so on. Such words have an effect of pleasure on the heart of the person to whom they are said. Every pleasant word is a charity and its reward is bestowed by Allāh the Almighty." (Sharh Riyādh Is-Sāliheen, 2/996, Chapter, "Recommendation of pleasant speech and meeting people with a cheerful face")

Non-timed Sunan

 Remembering Allāh in meetings and mentioning His name (i.e. praising Him).

Abu Hurayrah narrated that the Prophet said, "Allāh has angels who go about on roads and paths looking for those who remember Allāh and mention His name. When they find some people remembering Allāh and mentioning His name, they call each other saying, 'Come to what you are looking for.'." He added, "The angels then surround them with their wings until the space between them and the lowest sky is fully covered ..." (Al-Bukhāriy no. 6408, Muslim no. 2689)

 Concluding meetings with "Kaffārat Il-Majlis" (i.e. Expiation of meetings).

Abu Hurayrah narrated that the Prophet said, "Whoever sits in a meeting and utters a lot of prattle, but says before getting up,

« سُبْحَانَكَ اللَّهُمَّ وَبِحَمْدِكَ أَشْهَدُ أَن لاَ إِلَهَ إِلاَّ أَنْتَ، أَسْتَغْفِرُكَ وَأَتُوبُ إِلَيْكَ »

'Glory and Praise be to You, O Allāh. I bear witness that there is no God but You. I ask You for Your forgiveness, and I turn to You in repentance.', any sins that he may have committed during this meeting will be forgiven." (At-Tirmidthiy no. 3433, and it was graded as Saheeh (Authentic) by Shaykh Al-Albāniy, may Allāh have mercy on him.)

Non-timed Sunan

Third: Sunan of Dress and Adornment

 Starting with the right foot when putting shoes on.

It is Sunnah for a Muslim when putting his shoes on to start with the right foot first, and when taking them off to start with the left foot first.

Abu Hurayrah ؓ narrated that Allāh's Messenger ﷺ said, "When any one of you puts his shoes on, he should begin with the right foot first, and when he takes them off,

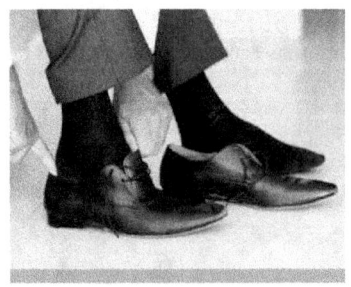

he should begin with the left foot first, so that the right shoe will be the first to be put on and the last to be taken off." (Al-Bukhāriy no. 5856)

Imām Muslim reported the Hadeeth of *Abi Hurayrah* ؓ in which he narrated that the Prophet ﷺ said, "One of you should not walk in one sole (i.e. sandal or shoe). He should rather put them both on, or take them both off." (Muslim no. 2097)

Non-timed Sunan

Thus, three Sunan are mentioned in these two Ahādeeth:

1. Starting with the right foot when putting shoes on.
2. Starting with the left foot when taking shoes off.
3. Either putting both shoes on or taking both off, avoiding walking with only one shoe on, as this is prohibited.

Wearing white clothes.

It is Sunnah to wear white clothes.

Ibn 'Abbāss narrated, "The Messenger of Allāh said, 'Wear white clothes, because they are the best of clothes, and use them for shrouding your dead.'." (Ahmad no. 2219, Abū Dāwood no. 3878 and At-Tirmidthiy no. 994)

Shaykh Ubn 'Uthaymeen, may Allāh have mercy on him, said, "White clothes for men include shirts, wraparounds, and pants. However, if one wears another color, there is nothing wrong with that, provided that it is not something that resembles women's clothes." (The explanation of Riyādh As-Sāliheen, 2/1087)

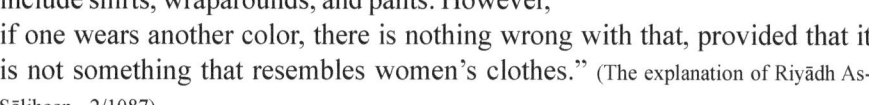

Using perfume (for men).

Anass narrated that the Prophet mentioned that one of the things that have been made dear to him among the pleasures of this world is perfume. (Ahmad no. 12293 and *An-Nasā'iy* no. 3940)

Moreover, *'Ā'ishah*, may Allāh be pleased with her, narrated that Allāh's Messenger extremely disliked that any unpleasant odor should emit from him." (Al-Bukhāriy no. 6972)

Non-timed Sunan

4 It is disliked to refuse a gift of perfume.

This is proven by the following Hadeeth:

Anass Ubn Mālik reported, "The Prophet used to not refuse a gift of perfume." (Al-Bukhāriy no. 2582)

5 Starting with the right side when combing the hair.

This is proven by the following Hadeeth:

'Ā'ishah, may Allāh be pleased with her, narrated, "Allāh's Messenger used to like starting with the right side when putting his shoes on, combing his hair, purifying himself, and in all of his affairs." (Al-Bukhāriy no. 168, Muslim no. 268)

Non-timed Sunan

Fourth: Sunan of Sneezing and Yawning

Sunan of Sneezing:

1 Saying "Al-Hamdu Lillāh" (Praise is due to Allāh) after sneezing, being replied "Yarhamuk Allāh", then replying "Yahdeekum Ullah wa Yuslihu Bālakum".

Abu Hurayrah narrated that the Prophet said, "If one of you sneezes, he should say 'Al-Hamdu Lillāh' (i.e. Praise is due to Allāh), and his brother or companion should say to him 'Yarhamuk Allāh' (i.e. May Allāh bestow His Mercy on you). When the latter says 'Yarhamuk Allāh,' the former should say 'Yahdeekum Ullah wa Yuslihu Bālakum' (i.e. May Allāh give you guidance and grant you well-being)." (Al-Bukhāriy no. 6224)

It is also Sunnah to change the wording occasionally, saying "Al-Hamdu Lillāhi *'Ala* Kulli Hāl" (i.e. Praise be to Allāh in all circumstances).

This is indicated by the Hadeeth narrated by Abi Dāwood, in which the Prophet said, "If one of you sneezes, he should say, 'Al-Hamdu Lillāh *'Ala* Kulli Hāl' (i.e. Praise be to Allāh in all cirumstances)." (Abū Dāwood no. 5031).

Non-timed Sunan

Any one who hears the one who sneezed saying "Al-Hamdu Lillāh" should reply, "Yarhamuka Allāh" (i.e. May Allāh bestow His Mercy on you), and it is Sunnah for the one who sneezed to reply to that saying, "Yahdeekum Ullah wa Yuslihu Bālakum" (i.e. May Allāh give you guidance and grant you well-being).

Anass said, "Two men sneezed in the presence of the Prophet, and the Prophet answered one of them 'Yarhamuk Allāh,' and did not answer the other one. The latter said, 'O Messenger of Allāh, you replied to him "Yarhamuka Allāh," but you did not reply to me.' The Prophet said, 'He praised Allāh, and you did not praise Allāh.'" (Al-Bukhāriy no. 6225)

In another Hadeeth, *Abu Moussa Al-Ash'ariy* reported that he heard the Messenger of Allāh say, "If one of you sneezes and then praises Allāh, respond to him with Tashmeet, and if he does not praise Allāh then do not respond to him with Tashmeet." (Muslim no. 2992)

Tashmeet is replying to one who sneezes by saying, "Yarhamuka Allāh" (i.e. May Allāh have mercy on you).

If however it is a matter of education, such as a father educating his son or a teacher educating his students, then the father or teacher can ask the child who sneezed to say "Al-Hamdu Lillāh", in order to educate him, as it might be that the child does not know this Sunnah.

Moreover, if someone has a cold and sneezes more than three times, then he should be answered "Yarhamuk Allāh" three times, but after the third time he should not be answered "Yarhamuk Allāh".

This is indicated in the Hadeeth of *Abi Hurayrah* who narrated the the Prophet said, "Answer your brother who sneezes, 'Yarhamuk Allāh' (i.e. May Allāh have mercy on you), three times. If however he sneezes more than than three times, then he has a cold." (Abū Dāwood no. 5034)

In another narration reported by Muslim, *Salamah Ubn Ul-Akwa'* narrated that when a man sneezed in the presence of the Prophet, *Salamah* heard the Prophet answering the man who sneezed, 'Yarhamuk Allāh' (i.e. May Allāh have mercy on you). *Salamah* continues that the man then sneezed again and the Messenger of Allāh said, "The man has a cold." (Muslim no. 2993)

Non-timed Sunan

Thus, one who sneezes should not be answered in two situations:

1. If the one who sneezes does not praise Allāh the Almighty after sneezing.

2. If someone sneezes more than three times and is thus expected to have a cold.

Sunan of Yawning:

- Resisting yawning as much as possible, or holding the hand over the mouth while yawning.

This is proven by the following Hadeeth:

Abu Hurayrah narrated that the Prophet said, "Allāh likes sneezing and dislikes yawning, so if someone sneezes and then praises Allāh, it is his right on every Muslim who heard him to answer him, 'Yarhamuk Allāh' (i.e. May Allāh have mercy on you). As for yawning, it is from Satan, so one should try his best to stop it. If one says 'Ha' while yawning, Satan laughs at him." (Al-Bukhāriy no. 2663)

Imām Muslim reports through *Abi Sa'eed* that the Prophet said, "When one of you yawns, he should hold his hand over his mouth, lest Satan enters therein." (Muslim no. 2995)

Thus, one should try to prevent yawning either by repressing it by closing his mouth or biting his lower lip or similar methods, or he should at least cover his mouth with his hand while yawning.

In addition, it is preferred for one who yawns to avoid raising his voice while yawning or making sounds like "Ha" or "Ah" or similar sounds, as this makes Satan laugh at him.

This is proven by the following Hadeeth:

Abu Hurayrah reported that the Prophet said, "Yawning is from Satan. Thus, one who yawns should try his best to stop it, and if one says 'Ha' while yawning, Satan laughs at him.'." (Al-Bukhāriy no. 3298, Muslim no. 2994)

Note: Some people are used to saying {أعوذ بالله من الشيطان الرجيم} "I ask Allāh's refuge against the cursed devil" after yawning. It should be noted that there is no valid evidence for this and it is not part of the Prophet's Sunnah, as the Prophet did not say this when he yawned.

Non-timed Sunan

 Fifth: Other Daily Sunan

 Dthikr of entering and leaving the bathroom.

 Dthikr of entering the bathroom:

One who enters the bathroom should say the Dthikr that is narrated in the following Hadeeth reported in Saheeh Al-Bukhāriy and Saheeh Muslim:

Anass said, "Whenever the Prophet entered the bathroom he would say, 'O Allāh, I seek refuge with you from Khubuth/Khubth and *Khabā'ith*.'." (Al-Bukhāriy no. 6322, Muslim no. 375)

Khubuth in Arabic (pronounced with letter u after the letter b) means male devils, and in this case *Khabā'ith* would mean female devils.

On the other hand, Khubth in Arabic (pronounced without letter u after the letter b) means evil, and in the this case *Khabā'ith* would mean evil-doers. This meaning according to the latter spelling is more general and is the most narrated by the scholars.

 Dthikr of leaving the bathroom:

'Ā'ishah, may Allāh be pleased with her, mentioned that when the Prophet ﷺ used to step out of the bathroom, he would say, "Ghufrānak" (i.e. I ask Your forgiveness, O Allāh). (Ahmad 6/155 no. 25220, Abū Dāwood no. 30, and At-Tirmidthiy no. 7)

 Preparing one's will.

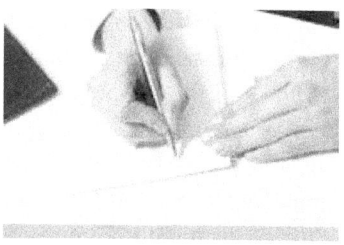

Preparing the will is an act of Sunnah during health and illness. The Prophet ﷺ says: "It is the duty of a Muslim who has something which is to be given as a bequest, not to let two nights pass without having his will written down with him." (Al-Bukhāriy no. 2783, Muslim no. 1626)

By "two nights" the Prophet ﷺ means to symbolize for a short period of time, not specifically two nights. This has been stressed on because no one knows exactly when they will die.

As for the rights of Allāh Almighty regarding Zakat, Hajj, or any sort of Kaffārah (i.e. expiation), in addition to people's rights regarding debts, they are obligatory and not just Sunnah, so one must write them down in his will, especially if no one knows about them, and there is a rule in `Principles of Fiqh` that states, "Whatever thing an obligation cannot be accomplished without, is an obligation."

 Kindness and leniency in buying and selling.

Both the purchaser and the seller should deal with each other leniently and avoid harshness, debate on prices, etc.

Non-timed Sunan

This is proven by the following Hadeeth:

Jābir Ubn 'Abdillāh said that the Prophet said, "May Allāh's mercy be on him who is lenient when he buys, when he sells, and when he demands his money." (Al-Bukhāriy no. 2076)

The same applies when one asks for any of his rights. It is Sunnah to be lenient and tolerant as the Prophet said, "... and when he demands his money."

 Praying two *Rak'ahs* after performing ablution.

This is from the daily Sunan that have great virtue and entail great reward. *Abu Hurayrah* reported that the Prophet once said to *Bilāl* at the time of Fajr prayer, "*Bilāl*, tell me about the act you have done that you deem would be the most rewarding for you with Allāh, for I heard the sound of your footsteps in front of me in Paradise."
Bilāl replied, "I have not done a deed that I deem would be the most rewarding for me with Allāh, except that I have never performed ablution during any hour of night or day unless I offered prayer with that purification as much as Allāh has written for me to pray." (Al-Bukhāriy no. 1149, Muslim no. 2458)

 Waiting for prayer.

Waiting for prayer is a Sunnah that has a great virtue and entails great reward.

Abu Hurayrah said that the Prophet said, "One is considered in prayer as long as he is waiting for prayer, and nothing but the prayer is preventing him from going to his family." (Al-Bukhāriy no. 659, Muslim no. 649)

Thus, Muslims are rewarded for waiting for prayer exactly as they are rewarded for the prayer itself.

Abu Hurayrah said that the Prophet said: "The angels pray for every one of you as long as he remains in the place in which he prayed and does not break his *Wudū'* (ablution). The angles say, 'O Allāh, forgive him. O Allāh, have mercy to him.'." (Al-Bukhāriy no. 659, Mulsim no. 649)

In another narration by Imām Muslim it says, "… as long as he neither hurts anybody nor invalidates his ablution." (Muslim no. 649)

Thus, this reward is conditional, and the condition is to avoid doing any harm to others and to avoid invalidating *Wudū'*.

 ### Siwāk (Tooth-stick).

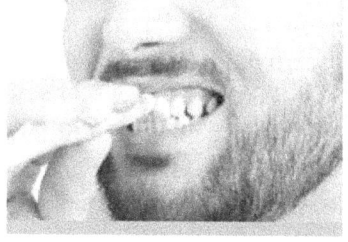

Siwāk is from the Sunan that may be done at anytime. The Prophet ﷺ persistently urged us to use it. *Anass* narrated that the Prophet ﷺ said: "I have indeed urged you regarding Siwāk." (Al-Bukhāriy no. 888)

'Ā'ishah, may Allāh be pleased with her, narrated that the Prophet ﷺ said: "Siwāk cleanses the mouth and pleases the Lord." (Ahmad no. 7 and *An-Nasā'iy* no. 5)

Using Siwāk is most recommended in certain situations such as upon night prayer, upon *Wudū'*, before every prayer, and on entering one's home, and Allāh knows best.

 ### Renewal of *Wudū'* for every prayer.

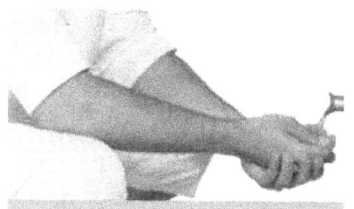

It is Sunnah to renew *Wudū'* for every prayer. If a Muslim has made *Wudū'* for Maghrib prayer and is still maintaining his state if *Wudū'* when *'Ishā'* time comes in, it is Sunnah to perform *Wudū'* again at *'Ishā'* time.

This is proven by the following Hadeeth:

Al-Bukhāriy reported, "The Prophet ﷺ used to make *Wudū'* for every prayer." (Al-Bukhāriy no. 214)

It is also Sunnah for a Muslim to maintain his state of *Wudū'* during the day. *Thawbān* said that the Prophet ﷺ said, "No one maintains his state of *Wudū'* except a believer." (Ahmad no. 22434, Ibn Mājah no. 277, and Ad-Dārimiy no. 655)

Non-timed Sunan

Sunan of *Du'ā'* (Supplication).

1. Making *Du'ā'* while in a state of Tahārah (Purity).

Both Al-Bukhāriy and Muslim reported in their Saheehs the Hadeeth of *Abi Moussa Al-Ash'ariy* and his story with his uncle *Abi 'Āmer* when the Prophet sent him in lead of the army of Awttās. The Hadeeth says, "*Abu 'Āmer* was killed and he asked *Abā Moussa* to convey his greetings to the Prophet, and to ask for the Prophet's *Du'ā'* for him. *Abu Moussa* said, 'I told the Prophet about *Abi 'Amer*'s story and request.' Allāh's Messenger then asked for water and made ablution from it. He then raised his hands and said, 'O Allāh, I ask You for forgiveness to *Abi 'Āmer*.' Abu Moussa said, 'He raised his hands while making *Du'ā'* to the extent that I saw the whiteness of his armpits.' The Prophet then said, 'O Allāh, raise his rank on the day of judgment above many of mankind.'." (Al-Bukhāriy no. 4323, Muslim no. 2498)

2. Facing the Qiblah (Direction of the *Ka'bah*).

Abdullāh Ibn 'Abbāss narrated, "*'Umar Ubn Ul-Khattab* said, 'When it was the day of the battle of Badr, the Messenger of Allāh took a glance at the Mushrikeen, who were one thousand, while his own companions were three hundred and nineteen men. The Prophet turned towards the Qiblah, then he extended his hands and began his supplication to his Lord, "O Allāh, accomplish for me what you have promised me. O Allāh, bring about what have promised me. O Allāh, if this small group of Muslims is perished, You will not be worshiped on this earth." He continued his supplication to his Lord extending his hands and facing the Qiblah until his cloak slipped down off his shoulders. *Abu Bakr* then came to him, picked up the cloak and placed it on his shoulders, and then embraced him from behind and said, "Prophet of Allāh, this prayer of yours to your Lord is sufficient, and He will fulfill for you what He has promised you.".'." (Muslim no. 1763)

3. Raising both hands.

The evidence for this can be found in the previous Hadeeth narrated by *Ibn 'Abbāss*, "… and Allāh's Messenger faced the Qiblah, and then he extended his hands and raised them …" (Muslim no. 1763)

Non-timed Sunan

4) Starting *Du'ā'* by praising Allāh, the Almighty, then asking Allāh to send peace and blessings upon his Prophet ﷺ.

At-Tirmidthiy reported through *Fadhālah Ibn 'Ubaid* that he said, "While the Prophet ﷺ was sitting, a man entered and prayed and then said, 'O Allāh, forgive me and have mercy on me.' The Prophet ﷺ told him, 'You were hasty. When you supplicate, praise Allāh with what He deserves and ask Him to pray on me, then ask Allāh for what you need.'." (At-Tirmidthiy no. 3476)

5) Making *Du'ā'* with the ninety nine names of Allāh, the Almighty.

A person should choose the name of Allāh the meaning of which corresponds to his need. If one is asking Allāh for livelihood, it would be adequate to say, "O Allāh, The Superb Provider." If one is asking Allāh for mercy, it would be adequate to say, "O Allāh, The Most Merciful." If one is asking Allāh for dignity, it would be adequate to say, "O Allāh, the Almighty." If one is asking Allāh for forgiveness, it would be adequate to say, "O Allāh, the Ever-Forgiving," and so on.

Thus, he should supplicate with what is appropriate. Allāh Almighty says:

﴿ وَلِلَّهِ الأَسْمَاءُ الْحُسْنَى فَادْعُوهُ بِهَا ﴾

"Allāh has the most beautiful names, so call upon Him by His names ..." (*Soorat Ul-A'rāf*, Verse 180)

6) Repetition and insistence in *Du'ā'*.

Ibn 'Abbāss narrated in the Hadeeth quoted earlier, that the Prophet ﷺ said, "O Allāh, accomplish for me what You have promised me. O Allāh, bring about what You have promised me." He continued his supplication to his Lord, extending his hands and facing the Qiblah, until his cloak slipped down off his shoulders. *Abu Bakr* then came to him, picked up his cloak and placed it on his shoulders and then embraced him from behind and said, "Prophet of Allāh, this prayer of yours to your Lord is sufficient, and He will fulfill for you what He has promised you." (Muslim no. 1763)

In the Saheehayn, *Abu Hurayrah* narrated that the Prophet ﷺ made *Du'ā'* for the tribe of Dawss and said, "O Allāh guide Dawss and bring them to Islam, O Allāh guide Dawss and bring them to Islam." (Al-Bukhāriy no. 2937, Muslim no. 2524)

Non-timed Sunan

Imām Muslim also reports in his Saheeh, the Hadeeth about the man who would travel on a long journey and get disheveled and dusty, raising his hands to the sky saying 'O Lord! O Lord!' ... (Muslim no. 1015). This repetition in calling upon Allāh signifies urge and insistence.

It is Sunnah to make *Du'ā'* three times. This is taken from the Hadeeth of Ibn Mas'oud ؓ in which he narrates that the Prophet ﷺ called upon Allāh against Quraysh three times. (Al-Bukhāriy no. 240, Muslim no. 1794)

7> Making *Du'ā'* in secret.

Allāh, the Almighty, said,

﴿ ادْعُوا رَبَّكُمْ تَضَرُّعًا وَخُفْيَةً ﴾

"Call upon your Lord with humility and in secret. He does not like aggressors." (*Soorat Ul-A'rāf*, Verse 55)

Making *Du'ā'* in secret is closer to sincerity, and thus Allāh praised Zakariyyā when He, the Almighty, said,

﴿ إِذْ نَادَى رَبَّهُ نِدَاءً خَفِيًّا ﴾

"When he called out his Lord in secret." (*Soorat Maryam*, Verse 3)

Some scholars said that he called upon Allāh in secret because of sincerity.

Someone might say: What should I ask for in my *Du'ā'*?

One should make *Du'ā'* to ask for whatever he wants from the matters of this world or the Hereafter. It is best to use the supplications that are reported in the *Qur'ān* and the Sunnah, as they include all good of this world and the Hereafter. When the Prophet ﷺ was asked this question, he answered with great words that comprise all good of this world and the Hereafter, and what a generous gift and great glad-tiding this is for a Muslim. Thus, we need to take care of the supplications of the *Qur'ān* and the Sunnah and contemplate them.

Abu Mālik Il-Ashja'iy reports through his father, may Allāh be pleased with both of them, that he narrated that a man came to the Prophet ﷺ and said, "O Messenger of Allāh, What should I say when I call upon my Lord?" The Prophet ﷺ said, "Say, 'O Allāh, forgive me, have mercy on me, give me well-

Non-timed Sunan

being and health in this life and in the Hereafter, and give me sustenance.'," and the Prophet ﷺ put together his fingers except the thumb and said, "This supplication gives you the good of both this life and the Hereafter." (Muslim no. 2697)

In another narration, it is reported that when someone converted to Islam, the Prophet would order him to use say words for supplication, "O Allāh, Forgive me, show mercy upon me, guide me, give me well-being, and give me sustenance." (Muslim no. 2697)

 Note: It is Sunnah to pray for your brother in his absence, which is an accepted *Du'ā'* by the will of Allāh. One who does this is greatly rewarded. Imām Muslim reported in his Saheeh through *Abi d-Dardā'* ؓ that the Prophet ﷺ said, "The *Du'ā'* of a person for his Muslim brother in his absence is an answered one. At his head there is an appointed angel, and every time he prays for his Muslim brother, the angel says, 'Āmeen, may you have likewise.'." (Muslim no. 2733)

◆ Everyone is in serious need for private seclusion to hold himself accountable and remember Allāh, especially when negligence and preoccupation are widespread.

Non-timed Sunan

Remembrance of Allāh (Dthikr).

The greatest Dthikr is reciting the *Qur'ān*, which is an act of worship that made our ancestors stay awake long at night.

﴿ كَانُوا قَلِيلاً مِّنَ اللَّيْلِ مَا يَهْجَعُونَ . وَبِالْأَسْحَارِ هُمْ يَسْتَغْفِرُونَ ﴾

"They used to sleep only little in the night, and they used to be found calling up on their Lord asking for forgiveness late in the night before dawn." (*Soorat Ud-Dthāriyāt*, Verse 18). Thus, in their night, they would do both acts of worship, reciting the *Qur'ān*, and supplicating with the Adthkār of the Sunnah. Imagine how great a night filled with worship and supplication is, and imagine the loss of those who fill their nights with useless deeds or sins, may Allāh grant us guidance.

Hammād Ibn Zayd said that *'Atā' Ibn Il-Sa'ib* said that *Abā Abd Ir-Rahmān* said, "We took the *Qur'ān* from people who told us that when they would learn ten verses of the *Qur'ān*, they would not move to the following verses until they had applied the first ten verses in their lives. Thus, we used to learn the *Qur'ān* and learn how to act accordingly. Yet, some people will come after us who would superficially read the *Qur'ān* with their tongues and not apply it in their lives." (*Siyar A'lām An-Nubalā'*, 4/269)

Dthikr revives the heart.

In our current days, many people complain about the stiffness of their hearts due to their busyness with this worldly life, and thus their hearts do not pay the appropriate attention to the remembrance of Allāh. In fact life of the heart and tranquility cannot be achieved except with the remembrance of Allāh.

In a Hadeeth reported in Saheeh Il-Bukhāriy, *Abu Moussa Al-Ash'ariy* narrated that the Prophet said, "One who remembers his Lord compared to one who does not remember his Lord, is like the living compared to the dead." In Muslim's narration, "A house in which Allāh's name is remembered compared to a house in which Allāh's name is not remembered, is like the living compared to the dead." (Al-Bukhāriy no. 6407, Muslim no. 779)

Non-timed Sunan

Allāh urges us in many verses to have the habit of remembrance of Allāh and mentioning His name (i.e praising Him).

« يَا أَيُّهَا الَّذِينَ آمَنُوا اذْكُرُوا اللَّهَ ذِكْرًا كَثِيرًا. وَسَبِّحُوهُ بُكْرَةً وَأَصِيلًا »

"O you who believe, remember Allāh very often, and glorify Him morning and evening." (*Soorat Ul-Ahzāb*, Verse 42)

Allāh promised to forgive those who remember Him and mention His name, and give them great reward.

« وَالذَّاكِرِينَ اللَّهَ كَثِيرًا وَالذَّاكِرَاتِ أَعَدَّ اللَّهُ لَهُم مَّغْفِرَةً وَأَجْرًا عَظِيمًا »

"… and those of men and women who remember Allāh often, for all of them Allāh has prepared forgiveness and great reward." (*Soorat Ul-Ahzāb*, Verse 35)

Allāh warned us of being like hypocrites who rarely remember Allāh.

« إِنَّ الْمُنَافِقِينَ يُخَادِعُونَ اللَّهَ وَهُوَ خَادِعُهُمْ وَإِذَا قَامُوا إِلَى الصَّلَاةِ قَامُوا كُسَالَى يُرَاؤُونَ النَّاسَ وَلَا يَذْكُرُونَ اللَّهَ إِلَّا قَلِيلًا »

"Verily, hypocrites seek to deceive Allāh, but it is He Who causes them to be deceived, and when they stand up for prayer they do so in laziness, only to be seen by people, but little do they remember or praise Allāh." (*Soorat Un-Nisā'*, Verse 142)

Allāh warned us of paying full attention to money and offspring, and forgetting Allāh the Almighty.

« يَا أَيُّهَا الَّذِينَ آمَنُوا لَا تُلْهِكُمْ أَمْوَالُكُمْ وَلَا أَوْلَادُكُمْ عَن ذِكْرِ اللَّهِ وَمَن يَفْعَلْ ذَٰلِكَ فَأُولَٰئِكَ هُمُ الْخَاسِرُونَ »

"O you who believe, let not your properties or your children divert you from the remembrance of Allāh, and whosoever does that then they are the losers." (*Soorat Ul-Munāfiqoon*, Verse 9)

Imagine this great reward:

Allāh, the Almighty, said,

« فَاذْكُرُونِي أَذْكُرْكُمْ »

"Thus, remember Me (i.e. by mentioning my name during praying, glorifying, etc.) and I will remember you." (*Soorat Ul-Baqarah*, Verse 152)

In addition, Allāh said in the Qudsiy Hadeeth, "I am just as My slave thinks of Me (i.e. I am able to do for him what he thinks I can do for him), and I am with him when He remembers Me. If he remembers Me in himself, I remember him in Myself, and if he remembers Me in a group of people, I remember him in a group that is better than them." (Al-Bukhāriy no. 7405, Muslim no. 2675)

Other Valuable Daily Adthkār of Sunnah.

  Abu Hurayrah narrated that Allāh's Messenger said, "Whoever says a hundred times in one day, "None has the right to be worshiped but Allāh alone, Who has no partners, to Him belongs the kingdom and to Him belong all Praises, and He has power over all things (i.e. Omnipotent)," will get the reward of freeing ten slaves, a hundred good deeds will be written in his account, a hundred bad deeds will be erased from his account, he will be protected from Satan from the morning till the evening, and nobody will be superior to him except one who has done more than that which he has done. Whoever says, 'Subhān Allāh wa Bihamdih,' (i.e. Glory and Praise be to Allāh) a hundred times a day, all of his sins will be forgiven even if they were as much as the foam of the sea." (Al-Bukhāriy no. 3293, Muslim no. 2691)

Abu Ayyoob narrated that Allāh's Messenger said, "Whoever says, 'There is no God but Allāh alone, Who has no partner, His is the kingdom and His is the praise, and He has power over all things' ten times, will get the reward of freeing four slaves from the children of Ismaʿeel." (Al-Bukhāriy no. 6404, Muslim no. 2693)

Saʿd Ubn Abi Waqqāss narrated, "We were sitting with Allāh's Messenger and he said, 'Is any one of you incapable of earning one thousand rewards every day?' Someone from the people in the gathering asked, 'How can any one of us earn a thousand rewards?' Prophet Muhammad said, 'By Glorifying Allāh (i.e. saying "Subhān Allāh") a hundred times, one will be granted a thousand rewards, or will get a thousand sins wiped off his record.'." (Muslim no. 2698)

Abu Hurayrah narrated that Allāh's Messenger said, "Whoever says, "Glory and Praise be to Allāh" a hundred times in a day, all of his sins will be forgiven even if they were as much as the foam of the sea." (Al-Bukhāriy no. 6405, Mulsim no. 2692)

Non-timed Sunan

The Ahādeeth narrating various Adthkār and their virtues are so many. The ones that were quoted above are the most known and the authentic ones. Yet, there are many other Ahādeeth that show the virtues of Adthkār.

Abu Moussa Al-Ash'ariy said, "Allāh's Messenger said to me, 'Shall I tell you about one of the treasures of Paradise?' I said, 'Sure.' The Prophet replied, 'There is no power nor might except with Allāh.'." (Al-Bukhāriy no. 4202, Muslim no. 2704)

Abu Hurayrah that Allāh's Messenger said, "Saying 'Glory be to Allāh, all praise is due to Allāh, there is no God but Allāh, and Allāh is the Greatest,' is dearer to me than all that the sun has risen upon (i.e. the whole world)." (Muslim no. 2695)

Furthermore, asking Allāh's forgiveness is a type of Dthikr. *Al-Aghar Ul-Muzaniyy* narrated that the Prophet said, "Sometimes I perceive a veil over my heart, and I supplicate Allāh for forgiveness one hundred times in a day." (Muslim no. 2702)

This is a deed of Allāh's Messenger. The Prophet also advised us to ask forgiveness, as reported by Muslim through *Al-Agharr* who said, "The Prophet said, 'Oh people, repent to Allāh, for indeed I repent to Allāh one hundred times every day.'." (Muslim no. 2702)

Al-Bukhāriy also reported through *Abi Hurayrah* that he heard the Prophet saying, "I swear by Allāh that I supplicate for Allāh's forgiveness and turn to Him in repentance more than seventy times a day." (Al-Bukhāriy no. 6307)

Thus, a Muslim should not forget to continuously ask for Allāh's forgiveness.

Finally, I would like to conclude the Sunan of Dthikr (and all daily Sunan as well) with the following great Dthikr:

Abu Hurayrah narrated that Allāh's Messenger said, "Two words are light on the tongue, but weigh heavy in the balance, and are loved by the Allāh the Most Merciful, 'Glory and Praise be to Allāh. Glory be to Allāh, the Supreme.'." (Al-Bukhāriy no. 6406, Muslim no. 2694)

Praise be to Allāh, by Whose favors good deeds are accomplished.

www.ingramcontent.com/pod-product-compliance
Lightning Source LLC
LaVergne TN
LVHW020437070526
838199LV00063B/4766